Edmond Plauchut

China and the Chinese

Edmond Plauchut

China and the Chinese

ISBN/EAN: 9783337004057

Printed in Europe, USA, Canada, Australia, Japan

Cover: Foto ©ninafisch / pixelio.de

More available books at **www.hansebooks.com**

CHINA AND THE CHINESE

BY

EDMUND PLAUCHUT

TRANSLATED AND EDITED

BY

Mrs. ARTHUR BELL (N. D'Anvers)
AUTHOR OF 'THE ELEMENTARY HISTORY OF ART,' 'LIFE OF GAINSBOROUGH,'
'THE SCIENCE LADDERS,' ETC.

WITH FIFTY-EIGHT ILLUSTRATIONS

LONDON
HURST AND BLACKETT, LIMITED
13 GREAT MARLBOROUGH STREET
1899

TRANSLATOR'S NOTE

THIS brightly written little book by the well-known French author, Edmund Plauchut, who has spent many years in China, is the first of the new series known as the "Livres d'or de la Science" recently commenced by MM. Schleicher Frères of Paris. It gives in a succinct form a very complete account of the Chinese, both past and present, their religion, their literature, and their time-honoured customs. Touching but lightly on the many vexed questions of modern diplomacy, it yet presents a very true picture of the problems European statesmen have to solve in connection with the inevitable partition of the Celestial Empire, and will, it is hoped, be found of real service to those who wish to be abreast with the times, yet who have not the leisure to read the longer and more exhaustive books on the subject which are continually appearing.

NANCY BELL.

Southbourne-on-Sea,
May 1899.

CONTENTS

CHAPTER I

PAGE

The delight of exploring unknown lands—Saint Louis and the Tartars of olden times—The Anglo-French force enters Pekin—Terror of the "Red Devils"—The "Cup of Immortality"—The "Sons of Heaven"—Hong-Kong as it was and is—The Treaty of Tien-tsin—The game of "Morra"—First Tea-party in the Palace of Pekin—Chinese agriculture and love of flowers—Chinese literati—An awkward meeting between two of them—Love of poetry in China—Voltaire's letter to the poet-king—The Chinese army—The *Shu-King*, or sacred book of China—Yao and his work—Chung, the lowly-born Emperor—The Hoang-Ho, or "China's Sorrow"—Yu the engineer and his work—Chung chooses Yu to reign after him—The foundation of the hereditary monarchy in China 1

CHAPTER II

Trip up the Shu-Kiang river—My fellow-passengers and their costumes—A damaged bell—Female peasants on the river-banks—I am caught up and carried off by a laughing virago—Arrival at Canton—Early trading between China and Ceylon and Africa, etc.—The Empress Lui-Tseu teaching the people to rear silk-worms—The treaties of Nanking and Tien-tsin—Bombardment of Canton—Murder of a French sailor and terrible revenge—M. Vaucher and I explore Canton—The *fêtes* in honour of the Divinity of the North and of the Queen of Heaven—General appearance of Canton—An emperor's recipe for making tea—How tea is grown in China

—The Fatim garden—A dutiful son—Scene of the murder of the Tai-Ping rebels—The Temple of the five hundred Genii—Suicide of a young engineer—Return of his spirit in the form of a snake 33

CHAPTER III

General Tcheng-Ki-Tong and his book on China—The monuments of China—Those the Chinese delight to honour—A Chinese heroine—Ingredients of the "Cup of Immortality"—Avenues of colossal statues and monsters in cemeteries—Imperial edict in honour of K'wo-Fan—Proclamation of the eighteenth century—The Emperor takes his people's sins upon himself—Reasons for Chinese indifference to matters of faith—Lao-Tsze, or the old philosopher—His early life—His book, the *Tao-Teh-King*—His theory of the creation—Affinity of his doctrine with Christianity—Quotations from his book . . 57

CHAPTER IV

Lao-Tsze and Confucius compared—The appearance of Kilin, the fabulous dragon, to the father of Confucius—Early life of the Philosopher—The death and funeral of his mother—His views on funeral ceremonies—His visit to the King of Lu and discourse on the nature of man—Confucius advocates gymnasium exercises—His love of music—His summary of the whole duty of woman—He describes the life of a widow—He gives a list of the classes of men to be avoided in marriage—The seven legitimate reasons for the divorce of a wife—The three exceptions rendering divorce illegal—The missionary Gutzlaff's opinion of Confucius' view of woman's position—The Philosopher meets a man about to commit suicide—He rescues him from despair—He loses thirteen of his own followers 73

CHAPTER V

My voyage to Macao—General appearance of the port—Gambling propensities of the Chinese—Compulsory emigration—Cruel treatment of coolies on board ship—Disaster on the Paracelses reefs—The *Baracouns*—The grotto of Camoens—

CONTENTS

The *Lusiads*—Contrast between Chinese and Japanese—Origin of the yellow races: their appearance and language—Relation of the dwellers in the Arctic regions to the people of China—Russian and Dutch intercourse with the Celestials—East India Company's monopoly of trade—Disputes on the opium question—Expiration of charter—Death of Lord Napier of a broken heart—Lin-Tseh-Hsu as Governor of the Kwang provinces—The result of his measures to suppress trade in opium—Treaty of Nanking—War of 1856-1858—Treaty of Tien-tsin and Convention of Pekin—Immense increase in exports and imports resulting from them . . 97

CHAPTER VI

French aspirations in Tonkin—Margary receives his instructions—Work already done on the Yang-tse—Margary is insulted at Païl-Chou—He awaits instructions in vain at Lo-Shan—The Tung-Ting lake—A Chinese caravanserai—The explorer leaves the river to proceed by land—He meets a starving missionary—Kwei-Chou and the French bishop there—A terrible road—Arrival at the capital of Yunnan—Armed escort from Bhâmo—Meeting between Margary and Colonel Browne—Threatening attitude of natives—Margary crosses the frontier alone—Colonel Browne's camp surrounded—Murder of Margary outside Manwyne—Importance of Yunnan and Szechuan to Europeans 118

CHAPTER VII

Sir Thomas Wade demands his passports—Retires to man-of-war off Tien-tsin—Interviews with Li-Hung-Chang—Convention of Che-Foo—Description of Ichang on the Yang-tse—The Manchester of Western China—Pak-hoï and its harbour—A magnificent pagoda—Ceremony of opening the port to foreign trade—New Year's *fête* at Pak-hoï—The game of Morra—Description of Wenchow—Temples and pagodas turned into inns—Wahn and its native officials—Dislike of mandarins, etc., to missionaries—Beautiful surroundings of the town—An eclipse of the moon expected—The eclipse does not keep time—Excitement of the people—The dragon attacks the moon at last—Threatening message from the Emperor to the astronomers—Two astronomers beheaded in B.C. 2155—Reasons for importance attached to eclipses in China 135

CHAPTER VIII

I land at Shanghai—The Celestial who had never heard of Napoleon—Total value of exports and imports to and from Shanghai—What those exports and imports are—The devotion of the Chinese to their native land—The true yellow danger of the future—I am invited to a Chinese dinner at Shanghai—My yellow guests—The ladies find me amusing—Their small feet and difficulty in walking—A wealthy mandarin explains why the feet are mutilated—Sale of girls in China—Position of women discussed—A mandarin accepts a Bible—Our host takes us to a flower-boat—Description of boat—My first attempt at opium-smoking—A Celestial in an opium dream . 151

CHAPTER IX

Great commercial value of opium—Cultivation of the poppy—Exports of opium from India—What opium is—Preparation of the drug—Opinions on the English monopoly of the trade in it—Ingenious mode of smuggling opium—Efforts of Chinese Government to check its importation—Proclamation of the Viceroy Wang—Opinion of Li-Shi-Shen on the properties of opium—The worst form of opium smoking—Its introduction to Formosa by the Dutch—Depopulation of the island—Punishments inflicted on opium-smokers—Opinions of doctors on the effects of opium-eating or smoking—Chinese prisoners deprived of their usual pipe—The real danger to the poor of indulgence in opium—Evidence of Archibald Little—The Chinese and European pipe contrasted 166

CHAPTER X

Missionary effort in China—First arrival of the Jesuits—Landing of Michael Roger—Adam Schaal appointed Chief Minister of State—The scientific work of the Jesuits—Affection

CONTENTS

of the young Emperor Kang-Hi for them—Arrival of other monks—Fatal disputes between them and the Jesuits—The Pope interferes—Fatal results for the Christians—Speech of Kang-Hi—Expulsion of the Jesuits—Concessions to Europeans in newly-opened ports—Hatred of foreigners at Tien-tsin—Arrival of French nuns—Their mistakes in ignoring native feeling—Chinese children bought by the Abbé Chevrier—A Chinese merchant's views on the situation—Terrible accusations against the Sisters—Murder of the French Consul and his assistant—The Governor of Tien-tsin responsible—Massacre of the Abbé Chevrier and one hundred children—The Lady Superior and her nuns cut to pieces and burnt—The guilty Governor Chung-Ho sent to Paris as envoy—No proper vengeance exacted by the French—Other sisters go to Tientsin 184

CHAPTER XI

The Great Wall—Its failure as a defence—Forced labour—Mode of construction—Shih-Hwang-Ti orders all books to be burnt—Mandarins flung into the flames—The *Shu-King* is saved—How the sacred books came to be written—The sedan-chair and its uses—Modern hotels at Pekin—Examination of students for degrees—Cells in which they are confined—Kublai Khan conquers China—Makes Pekin his capital—Introduces paper currency—The Great Canal—Address to the three Philosophers—Marco Polo's visit to Pekin—His description of the Emperor—Kublai Khan's wife—Foundation of the Academy of Pekin—Hin-Heng and his acquirements—Death of Kublai Khan—Inferiority of his successors—Shun-Ti the last Mongol Emperor—Pekin in the time of the Mongols—When seen by Lord Macartney—The city as it is now 205

CHAPTER XII

Fall of the Mongol dynasty—The son of a labourer chosen Emperor—He founds the Ming dynasty—Choo becomes Taetsoo, and rules with great wisdom—He dies and leaves his kingdom to his grandson—Young-lo attacks and takes Nanking—The young Emperor burnt to death—Young-lo is proclaimed Emperor, and makes Pekin his capital—First European visits

China—Tartar chief usurps supreme power—Dies soon after—Foundation of present dynasty—Accession of Shun-Che—Chinese compelled to shave their heads—The old style of coiffure in China—Care of the modern pig-tail . . . 227

CHAPTER XIII

The Founder of the Ch'ing dynasty—A broken-hearted widower—The Louis XIV. of China—The Will of Kang-Hy—Young-t-Ching appointed his successor—The character of the new Emperor—Mission of Lord Macartney—He refuses to perform the Ko-too, or nine prostrations—Interview with Young-t-Ching—Results of the Mission to England—Accession of Kien-Long—He resolves to abdicate when he has reigned sixty years—Accession of Taou-Kwang—The beginning of the end—An adopted brother—War against China declared by England—The Pekin Treaty—Prince Hassan goes to visit Queen Victoria—The Regents and Tung-Che—Foreign Ministers compel the young Emperor to receive them . . 235

CHAPTER XIV

A child of four chosen Emperor—The power of the Empress Dowager—The Palace feud—The Palace at Pekin—A Frenchman's interview with the Emperor—The Emperor's person held sacred—Coming of age of the Emperor—An enlightened proclamation—Reception of the foreign ministers in 1889—Education of the young monarch—He goes to do homage at the tombs of his ancestors—A wife is chosen for him—His secondary wives—China, the battle-ground of the future—Railway concessions 251

LIST OF ILLUSTRATIONS

FIG.		PAGE
1.	VIEW OF HONG-KONG TAKEN FROM ABOVE THE TOWN	3
2.	CHINESE SOLDIERS	5
3.	CHINESE WEAPONS	6
4.	CHINESE HELMET AND QUIVER	7
5.	A YOUNG CHINESE WOMAN	8
6.	A CHINESE COURTESAN	9
7.	HWANG-TIEN-SHANG-TI, THE GOD OF HEAVEN	11
8.	A CHINESE MANDARIN	15
9.	ANCIENT CHINESE COSTUMES	17
10.	ANCIENT CHINESE COSTUMES	18
11.	A YOUNG CHINESE POET	21
12.	A NAUGHTY PUPIL	28
13.	A CHINESE BRIDGE SPANNING THE HOANG-HO	31
14.	A PAGODA	34
15.	A STREET IN CANTON	40
16.	A WOMAN OF THE PEOPLE WITH HER BABY	41
17.	A CHINESE MANDARIN	42
18.	A GONG-RINGER	43
19.	A CHINESE ACTOR	44
20.	A CHINESE ACTOR IN A TRAGIC PART	47
21.	A VILLA NEAR CANTON	51
22.	GENERAL TCHENG-KI-TONG	58
23.	LAO-TSZE	67
24.	THE HOUSE IN WHICH CONFUCIUS WAS BORN	75
25.	PORTRAIT OF CONFUCIUS	76
26.	A FUNERAL PROCESSION IN CHINA	77
27.	CHINESE TOMBS	78

LIST OF ILLUSTRATIONS

FIG.		PAGE
28.	A CHINESE CEMETERY	80
29.	A YOUNG CHINESE MARRIED LADY	88
30.	A MARRIAGE PROCESSION	92
31.	A DESPERATE MAN	94
32.	THE TOMB OF CONFUCIUS	95
33.	CHINESE PEASANT CRUSHING RICE	122
34.	A CHINESE FERRYMAN	124
35.	A MANDARIN'S HOUSE	127
36.	PORTRAIT OF HIS EXCELLENCY LI-HUNG-CHANG	138
37.	ICHANG	141
38.	A CHINESE DYER AT WORK	143
39.	A CHINESE VISITING CARD	144
40.	A CHINESE RESTAURANT. AFTER THE REPAST	156
41.	A CHINESE JUNK	165
42.	AN OPIUM-SMOKER	179
43.	OPIUM PIPES	181
44.	REQUISITES FOR OPIUM-SMOKING	183
45.	A TEMPLE AT TIEN-TSIN	195
46.	THE GREAT WALL	206
47.	BURNING OF MANDARINS AND HISTORICAL DOCUMENTS, BY ORDER OF SHIH-KWANG-TI	209
48.	A STREET IN PEKIN	214
49.	NIGHT-WATCHMEN IN PEKIN	216
50.	A CHINESE GENERAL IN HIS WAR-CHARIOT	220
51.	PORCELAIN TOWER AT NANKING	222
52.	MONOLITHS AT THE ENTRANCE TO THE TOMBS OF THE MING EMPERORS	231
53.	CHINESE BRONZES	233
54.	PORTRAIT OF ONE OF THE CHINESE EMPERORS OF THE CH'ING DYNASTY, PROBABLY KIEN-LONG	242
55.	ONE OF THE REGENTS DURING THE MINORITY OF TUNG-CHE	249
56.	A CHINESE SEDAN-CHAIR AND BEARERS	255
57.	A BONZE TORTURING HIMSELF IN A TEMPLE, AFTER A CHINESE PAINTING	260
58.	THE TOWN AND BRIDGE OF FUCHAN	265

CHINA AND THE CHINESE

CHAPTER I

The delight of exploring unknown lands—Saint Louis and the Tartars of olden times—The Anglo-French force enters Pekin—Terror of the "Red Devils"—The "Cup of Immortality"—The "Sons of Heaven"—Hong-Kong as it was and is—The Treaty of Tien-tsin—The game of "Morra" —First Tea-party in the Palace of Pekin—Chinese agriculture and love of flowers—Chinese literati—An awkward meeting between two of them—Love of poetry in China— Voltaire's letter to the poet-king—The Chinese army—The *Shu-King*, or sacred book of China—Yao and his work— Chung, the lowly-born Emperor—The Hoang-Ho, or "China's Sorrow"—Yu the engineer and his work—Chung chooses Yu to reign after him—The foundation of the hereditary monarchy in China.

I DO not deny the happiness of a life spent beneath the shadow of the belfry of one's native place, in all the unruffled peace of one's own home, surrounded by one's own family; but, after all, what are such joys as these compared to those of the explorer who goes forth to meet the unknown ready for all that may betide, making fresh discoveries at every turn, gladly facing all dangers and rejoicing in the ever-changing, ever-widening horizon before him? Who would care to forego the joys of memory, the power of living over again in old age the adventures of youth, of seeing once more with the mind's eye the wonders of the far-distant lands visited when the mind was still buoyant, the sight still undimmed, the limbs still in all the vigour of manhood? Happy mortal indeed is he who, thoroughly imbued with the spirit of the discoverer, looks upon death itself not as the end of all things, but the threshold of a new world, the beginning of yet another journey fraught with the deepest interest, to a bourne all the more fascinating because of the deep mystery in which it is shrouded.

This was how I reasoned with myself when I was a mere lad eagerly devouring the accounts of the work of the great early explorers, Marco Polo, the Dupleix, La Pérouse, Bougainville, Dumont D'Urville, Christopher Columbus, Mungo Park, the Landers, etc., not to speak of Swift's fascinating romance *Gulliver's Travels*, and the yet more thrilling *Robinson Crusoe* of Defoe. Like all boys with vivid imaginations, I was fired with a longing to emulate all these heroes, and said to my mother: "I have made up my mind to be a sailor!"

My ardour was, however, quickly quenched when I saw my mother's beautiful eyes fill with tears at the thought of parting from me. This did not

FIG. 1.—VIEW OF HONG-KONG TAKEN FROM ABOVE THE TOWN

prevent me from leaving France a few years later, for I found myself whilst still quite a young man free to go whither I would, and I made up my mind to make many a long and interesting journey. Of course I expected to meet with dangers and misfortunes, but I felt sure that any such drawbacks would be more than counterbalanced by the grand sights it would be my privilege to witness. My anticipations were in every way fully realized, and if after wandering all over the world I refrain from saying with Terence: "I am a man, and nothing in the nature of man is strange to me;" it is merely because poets alone are privileged to speak with such egotistical assurance.

I had already spent a considerable time in Oceania and a few months in Egypt, when I landed at Hong-Kong on the very threshold of the ancient Chinese Empire, which, according to well-authenticated annals, is older even than the mighty and venerable Egypt of the Pharaohs. I went to China as much to study her past on the spot as to be one of the first to hail that transformation which, when I arrived, was already on the eve of its inauguration, and is now rapidly becoming an accomplished fact. There was, indeed, urgent need for haste if I wished to study that moribund China so long closed to Europeans before the great change came, and cared to gaze upon her far-stretching table-lands girt about by heights crowned with never-melting snow, ere their solitudes were broken in upon by the desecrating steam-engine, in districts whence in mediæval times great hordes of yellow-skinned, fierce-eyed barbarians, their long black hair floating on their shoulders, swept westward to devastate Europe.

In those days five hundred thousand Tartars

FIG. 2.—CHINESE SOLDIERS.

invaded Russia, took possession of Moscow, burnt Cracow, and penetrated as far as Hungary. Saint Louis of France, who was then on the throne, stood in the greatest dread of them, but this did not prevent him from making a joke about them, quoted by the Sieur de Joinville, which, considering the state of affairs at the time, speaks well for his pluck and sense of humour. "Mother," he said to Queen Blanche of Castille, "if these Tartars come here, we must make them go back to the Tartarus from which they come!"

Time, however, never fails to bring about the poetic justice of revenge. Six centuries after the

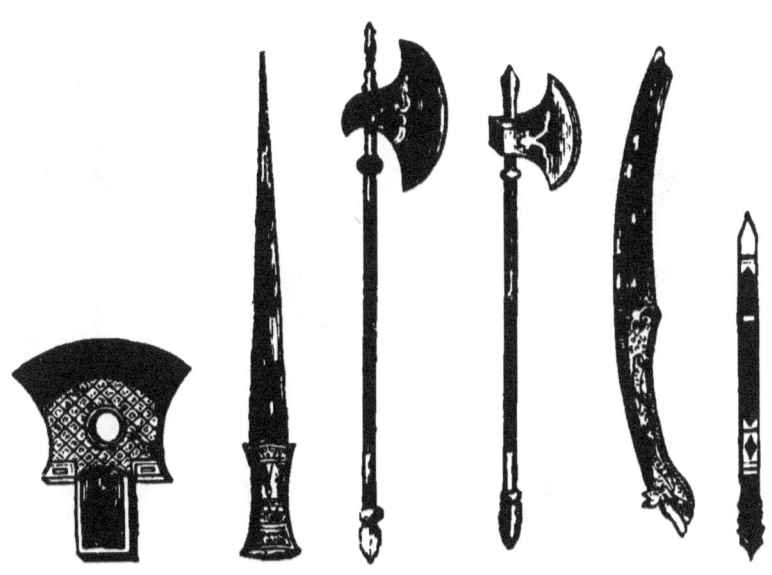

FIG. 3.—CHINESE WEAPONS.

sack of Cracow a little Anglo-French force entered Pekin with drums beating and flags flying, pillaged the Imperial Palaces, and returned to Europe laden with rich spoil. Chinese, Tartars, Mongols, and Manchus had all alike allowed themselves to be beaten by a mere handful of resolute men. What had they to oppose to European tactics, European weapons, and above all European discipline? Bows and arrows, old-fashioned muskets, spears, and shields adorned with fantastic designs. There was nothing for them to do but to run away; not that they were cowards, for they never have any fear of death, but simply because resistance was hopeless. Most of the generals in command of the army followed the usual custom in cases of defeat, and voluntarily emptied the bowl of poisoned opium to save themselves from being

FIG. 4.—CHINESE HELMET AND QUIVER.

triumphed over by their enemies. At Pekin, Canton, and many other centres of population in the vast Empire, the terrified women flung themselves into the wells to escape the violent death they expected the "red devils" would otherwise have inflicted on them. Only some forty years ago what did that immense multitude of Asiatic men and women know about us Europeans? Just about as much and no more than we did of them. One thing only is certain, that in the heroic days of the founders of the dynasty, from Hwang-Ti, the yellow Emperor, to Khiang-Luanh, the poet sovereign more than one ruler of China had drunk from the cup of immortality, that is to say, the cup of poison, rather than live to see the enemy enter his palaces as a conqueror. Enervated by a long course of self-indulgence, the Sons of Heaven, as the Emperors of China proudly style themselves, have degenerated terribly, and what with their own weakness and the arrogant encroachments of the eunuchs who guard the Imperial harem, many of the sovereigns would have been deposed, but for the intervention, now of an Empress-Dowager, now of some favourite wife, who, seizing the reins of power, has wielded the sceptre with virile strength and skill.

FIG. 5.—A YOUNG CHINESE WOMAN.

In 1851, when the English took possession of the island of Hong-Kong, it was but a rugged conical-shaped rock, dreary and forbidding in appearance. The Chinese then living on it were enraged at the intrusion of the foreigners, and one of them, the only baker on the island, resolved to dispose of all the intruders at one blow. He decided to poison them, and with this end in view he put arsenic into all the bread he supplied to the foreigners. He over-reached himself, for the dose was too strong, and suspicion was at once aroused. Those who tasted the bread escaped with violent sickness, and the English were not going to abandon the place for a reason so insignificant as that.

Hong-Kong is now a maritime port of the first rank, and its harbour is one of the finest and most beautiful in the whole world. The town boasts of hotels managed on the European system, and the slopes of the rocks are covered from the sea-shore to the highest point of the island with tasty villas. It is to opium, that other poison responsible for the death of so many Celestials, and as potent in its effects as the arsenic with which the patriotic baker tried to kill off all the foreigners, that Hong-Kong owes its immense prosperity. The French did much to aid the English in inaugurating that prosperity in 1857 and 1858, when they joined them as allies in the brief campaign which resulted in the taking of Canton and the signing of the celebrated Treaty of Tientsin. The various stipulations of that treaty, the full significance of which the Chinese do not seem to have realized at the time, included the right to

FIG. 6.—A CHINESE COURTESAN.

the allies of appointing diplomatic agents to the Court of Pekin, and the opening of five fresh ports to European commerce, whilst a strip of territory on the mainland, opposite to the island of Hong-Kong, was ceded to the British colony. The benefits which accrued to France were small, but the increase of British trade was enormous, and from that time to this the grand harbour has been one of the chief naval stations of the East.

In spite of its prosperity and importance, however, the town is anything but a pleasant place to stop in, and the foreign visitor soon gets tired of being jostled about by busy coolies and tipsy sailors. The great delight of the latter is to get drunk in the brandy-stores of Victoria Street, and then to dance, not, strange to say, with women, but without partners, to the music of a violin and a big drum. In the evening the floating and resident population alike resort in crowds to the opium-dens and houses of ill fame in the upper portions of the town. No one seems to feel any shame at being seen to enter these places, the windows of which are wide open, so that all can look into the brightly illuminated rooms, whence proceeds the sound of oaths in all manner of languages, whilst the loud clash of gongs mingles with the muffled songs of the Chinese beauties, and every now and then a shower of crackers is flung into the street below, bursting into zigzags of fire on the heads of the startled passers-by. In the eyes of the masters of the island, the intense commercial activity of the day atones for the dissipations of the night.

Contact with Europeans has, however, done little if anything to modify the ideas and customs of the Chinese. A few of the great native merchants, it is true, are willing now and then to drink a glass of champagne with the representatives of foreign houses, and teach them the game of Morra, which, strange to say, is to all intents and purposes the same as that played all over Italy, and is so well described by Mrs. Eaton in her *Rome in the Nineteenth Century*. " Morra," she says, "is played by the men, and merely consists in holding up in rapid succession any number of fingers they please, calling out at the same time the number their antagonist shows. . . . Morra seems to differ in no respect from the *Micure Digitis* of the Ancient Romans." If it be a fact, as some assert, that the various races of the world are more truly themselves in their games than in their work, this similarity in a pastime played by people so different as the Chinese and the Italians, would have a deep psychological significance.

FIG. 7.—HWANG-TIEN-SHANG TI, THE GOD OF HEAVEN.
(*In the Guimet Museum.*)

However that may be, drinking champagne and playing Morra together do not lead to any real friendship or intimacy between the Celestials and their hated foreign guests. There is not, and it seems as if there never could be, any true *rapprochement*, and this fact is at the root of the anxiety of statesmen for the future, in spite of the apparent progress made in the introduction of European ideas into the very stronghold of Chinese fanaticism, the Palace of Pekin, where a few months ago, on the occasion of her birthday, the Dowager Empress held that first reception of European ladies which was hailed by the European press as the commencement of a new era for China. An account of this historic tea-party may well be added here, for its being given was truly among the most remarkable events which have taken place in the century now so near its close. It seems that Lady Macdonald, the wife of the British Minister, was the prime mover in bringing about this startling innovation in the customs of the most conservative of all modern nations. The fact that it was the guests themselves who compelled the hostess to invite them, detracted not at all from the cordiality of their reception. Received at the entrance to the precincts of the Palace by numerous mandarins in brilliant costumes, the visitors were carried on State chairs to the electric tramway, strange anomaly in such a stronghold of retrogression as the capital of the Celestial Empire, and thence escorted to the audience-chamber by a group of ladies of the Court specially selected to attend them.

In the throne-room, the Empress and her unfortunate son, the nominal ruler of China, were seated side by side on a raised daïs, behind a table decorated with apples and chrysanthemums in the simple but effective Chinese manner. Presents and compliments were exchanged, a grand luncheon was served, over which the Princess Ching presided, and when tea was handed round later the Dowager Empress again appeared and sipped a little of the national beverage from the cup of each minister's wife. Finally, when the time for leave-taking came, the astute Dowager, giving way to an apparently uncontrollable burst of emotion, embraced all her visitors in turn. Time alone can prove whether this kiss were indeed one of peace or of future betrayal. In the eyes of the Court officials and their ladies it must have appeared far more startling than any of the political changes with which the air is rife.

The Chinese people, who know next to nothing of what is going on, and are more ignorant of the transformation taking place than even illiterate Europeans, are as indifferent to the past as to the future; they have been accustomed for centuries to obey unchanging laws of a wisdom acknowledged by even hostile critics; and startling innovation touching their own lives is the one thing which moves them out of their constitutional apathy.

Agriculture is the favourite occupation of the

Chinese, and they consider the tilling of the ground almost a religious duty. It has been customary for many ages for the supreme ruler to turn over a few furrows at the beginning of the agricultural year, that is to say the spring, and in all the provinces of the vast empire a similar ceremony is performed by the delegate of the Emperor. Flowers are everywhere cultivated, though generally in pots, with an enthusiasm amounting to passion, and marvellous skill is shown in the growing of dwarf trees, which produce quantities of fruit. In a word, vegetation in China is stamped with an originality setting it apart from that of any other country. In irrigation and the use of manure Chinese gardeners were long far in advance of western nations.

The chief ambition of every native of China is to leave behind him sons who on his death will give to his memory the homage he himself rendered to that of his own father, for it is in the reverence in which ancestors are held that the Chinese concentrate all their religious feeling. Even Shang-Ti, or the God of Heaven, Buddha, Lao-tsze, and Confucius only take secondary rank as compared with these ancestors.

The Literati, or scholars of China, have won their much-coveted distinction by many very severe examinations in the so-called *King*, or the five sacred books, and in the works of the great philosophers. Armed with the diploma securing to him the rank of a scholar, its fortunate possessor may aspire to the very highest functions of the empire. So very many win that diploma, however, and the numbers increase so rapidly every year, that, as in France and in England, there are not enough appointments for those qualified to receive them. In spite of this, the scholar even when out of place commands the respect of all who have not been promoted to the grade he has won. In his interesting account of his travels in Asia, Marcel Monnier gives a very pregnant illustration of the state of things I have been describing.

"As I was leaving the rampart," he says, "I witnessed a curious scene illustrative of the esteem in which—in this land where an hereditary aristocracy does not exist—is held the one ennobling rank, that of being the owner of a paper diploma. My bearers had just entered a very narrow causeway between two rice-fields, when they were suddenly brought to a halt by another chair coming from the opposite direction. This chair was occupied by a young man in elegant attire, wearing spectacles, and with a general air about him of being pleased with himself. Apparently he was a scholar fresh from examinations. The bearers on each side parleyed together, but neither seemed

FIG. 3.—A CHINESE MANDARIN.

disposed to yield place to the others. The discussion seemed likely to be interminable, when the scholar intervened, and addressing the chief of my bearers, shouted haughtily to him:

"'Why don't you get out of the way of a licentiate of Kan-Su?'

"My chief porter, a big sturdy fellow of about forty, did not move, but without budging an inch replied with equal haughtiness:

"'A licentiate? And of what year, pray?'

"Then without giving the other time to answer, he quickly dived into the little leather-bag hanging from his waist-band, brought out a greasy paper, and proudly unfolded it as if it were a flag, before the eyes of his astonished questioner.

"'Look!' he said.

"The young man took the paper with the very tips of his fingers, but he had scarcely glanced at the magic inscription on it before he handed it back with a respectful inclination of the head, at the same time ordering his men to withdraw. My porter, too, had his diploma, and he had had it for a long time. That of recent date had to give way to the earlier one. My chair passed on in triumph, whilst that of the newly-created scholar humbly waited at the side of the road in the rice-field."

The Chinese have the trading instinct as fully developed as have the descendants of Shem. They carry on commerce with the same wonderful *finesse*, the same keen eye for a bargain, and

CHINESE HONESTY

they are as fond of money as the Jews themselves. At the same time in really important affairs they are as much to be trusted, as thoroughly loyal to the other side, as any great merchant of the City

FIG. 9.—ANCIENT CHINESE COSTUMES.
(*Univers Pittoresque.*)

of London, or the *Rue du Sentier* in the French capital. These Chinese traders gave credit for enormous sums to the first foreign firms which had the audacity to found the Canton factories. On the faith of their signatures alone guaranteeing eventual payment, the heads of these foreign firms found themselves trusted with whole cargoes of tea and silks. After the failure of the Union Bank, of the *Comptoir national d'Escompte*, and certain great American houses, this giving of credit was

FIG. 10.—ANCIENT CHINESE COSTUMES.
(*Univers Pittoresque.*)

discontinued, but that it was ever granted remains a most significant fact. One proof of the extreme caution which succeeded the extraordinary confidence is, that there are no branches of the great Chinese firms of Shanghai and Hong-Kong in Paris, Marseilles, or Lyons. This is really no great loss, for the West will be invaded all too soon by the yellow races.

In Asia there are many more mystic dreamers and poets than is generally supposed. A Chinese mystic is called a bonze, or talapoin, the former word being of Japanese origin, introduced to China by Europeans. Women who devote themselves to a religious life are called bonzesses, but as certain abuses crept in of a kind which can readily be imagined, a very wise law was passed some time ago forbidding any woman to become a priestess till after her fortieth year, and certain censors have long advocated a yet further higher limit of age.

Amongst young women of the higher classes in the remote East, especially amongst those whose beauty destines them for the harem, poetry is held in high esteem. On the richly-lacquered screens and on the delicately-coloured fans so popular in China, are many representations of frail Chinese or Japanese beauties, tracing certain letters of the Mandarin alphabet with a fine pencil held in their tapering fingers with the characteristic pink nails. The words formed by these letters make up poetic phrases imbued with all the freshness and grace of the fair young girls who transcribe them. In them are sung the praises of the flowers of the hawthorn, the peach-tree, the sweetbriar, and even of a certain savoury tea. More than one Chinese Emperor has done homage to the Muses, and the most celebrated of these crowned poets was Khian-Lung, of the Tartar Manchu dynasty, who died at the end of the eighteenth century, and to whom Voltaire addressed the celebrated letter in verse of which the royal recipient was probably only able to understand, and that with considerable difficulty, the last few lines of which are quoted here:

> Receive, Celestial King, the compliments I write
> To one whose mighty throne stands on a double height!
> The western world knows well, in spite of all my crimes,
> I have a deep regard for monarchs who make rhymes.
> O thou whose soul is lit by Art's poetic fires,
> I pray thee tell me if your prosody requires
> That you in far Pekin, like us, must e'en submit
> To bind your thoughts in rules to make the tenses fit?
> Thus, if you choose to take the Alexandrine beat,
> Two equal lines must walk on six plain, equal feet,
> And so, one half for rhyme, the other for the sense,
> The whole of one great work to half you may condense!

The fame of two other Chinese poets, who flourished in the eighth century of our era, has also come down to us. These were Tchu-Fu and Li-Tai-Pé, who, as was Malherbe in France, were the first to reform poetry in their native land, laying down certain rules, which are still observed in the present day.

The peace enjoyed for so long a period by the country under consideration has led to the profession of arms being held of small account. Until quite recently all the "warriors" had to do was to put down local revolts, or to win for themselves a good drubbing from some aggrieved foreigner.

The weakness and defective organization of Asiatic armies is well known, and is proved afresh at every contact with a European force. The thorough inefficiency of that of China was forcibly brought out in the recent war with Japan, when the latter country showed itself to be so far in advance of its antagonist in every way. Nothing but drilling by European officers, for at least half a century, could make Chinese soldiers at all formidable to white troops. It is just the same with the people of the Corea, Annam, Tonquin, and Siam. It will, of course, be urged : but look at the Japanese, they too belong to the despised yellow races, yet have they not proved themselves able to organize a campaign? are they not full of warlike energy and martial ability? do they not also take high rank as imaginative

FIG. 11.—A YOUNG CHINESE POET.
(*Univers Pittoresque.*)

artists? In what do the white races excel? To all these queries we reply, the assumption that the Japanese belong to the same race as the yellow natives of the continent of Asia has to be proved. The children of the land of chrysanthemums and of the rising sun indignantly repel this hypothesis, and such authorities on ethnology as Kœmpfer, Golownin, Klaproth, and Siebold also reject it. Moreover, in this world everything is relative, and because the Japanese troops, armed with weapons of precision, were able to beat the badly-equipped Chinese forces, it does not follow that they could do the same if pitted against European soldiers. Whether they could or not still remains to be proved.

Before penetrating into the interior of the country, and studying the actual customs of the inhabitants at the present day, it will be well to glance back to the remote times when China first became a nation. Very interesting details of those early days have been preserved in the traditions of the Celestials, and from them we gather that the first dwellers in the land lived, as did so many of the races of Europe, in the forests, or in caves, clothing themselves in the skins of the wild beasts slain in the chase, whose flesh supplied them with food.

The first efforts at civilization appear to have been made in the North-west of the vast country, amongst the tribes camped on the banks of the Hoang-Ho, or Yellow River. The chiefs of these tribes gradually contracted the habit of making regular marriages, and living a home life with their families. To protect their wives and children they built huts; they discovered how to make fire, and with its aid to fashion agricultural implements and weapons. They knew how to distinguish plants good for food from those dangerous to human life; they fixed precise dates for the commencement of each of the four seasons; invented various systems of caligraphy, finally adopting the one still in use; and they acquired the art of weaving silk and cotton, which, according to the eminent sinologist, Leblois of Strasburg, recently deceased, they learnt from watching spiders at work.

Until the third century B.C. China was divided into small states, the weaker tributary to the stronger, the latter independent. The too-celebrated Emperor Thsin-Chi-Hwang-Ti, who two hundred years before the Christian era ordered the destruction by fire of all books, united the various little kingdoms into one, and it was only in his time that the Chinese Empire properly so called began. At this period, too, the name of Thsina, or China, originally that of the district governed by the incendiary, came to be given to the whole country.

The most important historical documents are those making up what is called the *Shu-King*, dating from about B.C. 500, and written by a certain Kwang-Tsen. This valuable book has been translated into French by P. Gaubil and L. Biot, and its history is very romantic. It was supposed that every copy had been burnt by the agents of Thsin-Chi-Hwang-Ti, but an old literate, Fu Chang by name, had learnt it by heart, and later, one copy engraved on pieces of bamboo was found hidden in the wall of an old house which was being pulled down.

This sacred book, which is indeed a literary treasure, is now more than 2300 years old, and it contains extracts from works yet more ancient, so that it is the very best guide in existence to the early history of China.

It begins with a description of a chief named Yao, who, according to official Chinese chronology, flourished some 2350 years before the Christian era. If the portrait is not flattered, Yao must have been a perfect man. He lived in the province now known as Chen-si, and, like some great illumination, he attracted to himself all the barbaric hordes in the neighbourhood. His first care was to teach them to honour the Shang Ti, or Tien, that is to say, the Supreme God. He also employed certain men to watch the course of the heavenly bodies, or rather to continue the study of the stars begun before his time, not from any curiosity as to the science of astronomy strictly so called, but that agriculturists might learn the right seasons for the work they had to perform. According to the *Shu-King* the year was already divided in China into 366 days, and these days into four very strictly-defined periods, beginning at the times enumerated below:

1. The day and night of equal length, marking the middle of the spring season, or what is now known in Europe as the Equinox.

2. The longest day, marking the middle of the summer, now called the summer solstice.

3. The day and night of equal length, marking the middle of the autumn.

4. The shortest day, marking the middle of the winter solstice.

Yao having asked for a man capable of aiding him to govern his people well, his own son was the first to be suggested as a suitable person, but he was rejected, the father saying: "He is deficient in rectitude, and fond of disputing." Another candidate was sent away because he did a great deal of unnecessary talking about things of no value, and pretended to be humble although his pride was really boundless. Then a certain Chung was brought forward, renowned for his virtues in spite of his obscure birth. Although he was the son of a blind father and of a wicked mother who treated him cruelly, whilst his brother was puffed up with excessive pride, Chung yet loyally performed his filial duties, and even succeeded as it were unconsciously in correcting the errors of his relations, and saving them from the commission of serious crimes. He was quoted as the greatest known example of the practice of that most honoured of all virtues in China, filial piety, which is looked upon by the Celestials as the source of every good action of justice and of humanity.

Chung therefore was chosen, and he did not disappoint the hopes Yao had founded upon his rectitude and ability. The sacred book praises the justice of his administration, and he succeeded Yao on that great ruler's death, proving that the hereditary principle was considered dangerous in China even at that remote date. He commenced his reign by offering to the Supreme God, and performed the customary ceremonies in honour of the mountains, the flowers and the spirits, then held in veneration. He took the greatest pains to ensure that justice should be done to all. It is evident that there were schools in his day, for he gave orders that nothing but the bamboo should be used for the correction of insubordinate pupils. Chung wished faults committed without malice prepense to be pardoned, but severe punishments to be inflicted on the incorrigible and on those who abused their strength or their authority. He was anxious, however, that judges under him should temper their justice with mercy.

The ministers of state had names suggesting a pastoral origin, for they were all called Mon, a word answering to our shepherd. When Chung gave them their appointments, he would say to them: "You must treat those who come from a distance with humanity, instruct those who are near to you, esteem and encourage men of talent, believe in the virtuous and charitable and confide in them, and lastly have nothing to do with those whose manners are corrupt." He would also say to them sometimes: "If I do wrong you must tell me of it; you would be to blame if you praise me to my face and speak differently of me when my back is turned."

The *Shu-King* tells us further that having appointed a man skilled in music to teach that art to the children of the great ones of his kingdom, Chung said to him: "See that your pupils are sincere and polite, ready to make allowances for others, obliging and sedate; teach them to be firm without being cruel; inculcate discernment, but take care that they do not become conceited." He appointed a censor to preside over public meetings where speeches were made, saying to him: "I have an extreme aversion for those who use inflammatory language; their harangues sow discord, and do much to injure the work of those who endeavour to do good; the excitement and the fears they arouse lead to public disorders."

Would it not be well for a similar formula to be pasted up in every place of public meeting at the present day?

Every three years Chung instituted an inquiry into the conduct of the officials in his dominions, recompensing those who had done well, and punishing those who had done ill. Few other sovereigns have merited the eulogy pronounced on Chung by one of his ministers: "His virtues, said the critic, are not tarnished by faults. In the care he takes of his subjects, he shows great moderation, and in his government his grandeur of soul is manifest. If he has to punish, *the punishment does not descend from parents to children;* but if he has to give a reward, the benefit extends to the descendants of those recompensed. With regard to involuntary errors, he pardons them without inquiring whether they are great or small. Voluntary faults, however apparently trivial, he punishes. In doubtful cases the penalty inflicted is light, but if a service rendered is in question, the reward is great. He would rather run the risk of letting a criminal escape the legal punishment than of putting an innocent person to death." The same minister thus defines a fortunate man: "He is one who knows how to combine prudence with indulgence, determination with integrity, reserve with frankness, humility with great talents, consistency with complaisance, justice and accuracy with gentleness, moderation with discernment, a high spirit with docility, and power with equity."

FIG. 12.—A NAUGHTY PUPIL.

The Hoang-Ho, or Yellow River, the mighty

stream which rises in Thibet and flings itself into the Gulf of Pechili after a course of some 3000 miles, had from time immemorial been the cause of constant and terrible catastrophes in the districts it traversed. Chung therefore sent for a talented engineer named Yu, and ordered him to superintend the work of making canals and embankments to remedy the evil. There had been a specially destructive inundation just before this appointment, and the sacred book contains Yu's own account of what he had accomplished, couched, it must be owned, in anything but modest terms. "When," he says, "the great flood reached to heaven; when it surrounded the mountains and covered the hills, the unfortunate inhabitants were overwhelmed by the waters. Then I climbed on to the four means of transport. I followed the mountains, and I cut through the woods. I laid up stores of grain and meat to feed the people. I made channels for the river, compelling them to flow towards the sea. In the country I dug canals to connect the rivers with each other. I planted seed in the earth, and by dint of work something to live upon was won from the soil."

The memory of these vast undertakings has remained engraven on the minds of the Chinese, and they still think of Yu with undying gratitude. For all that, however, the Hoang-Ho has continued to be a menace to the Empire, for in 1789, and again in 1819, it overflowed its banks, causing a considerable amount of damage to property, and killing countless numbers of the riverside population. Only twelve years ago the wayward river, justly called by the sufferers from its ravages "China's sorrow," burst its southern embankment near Chang-Chan in the inland province of Shen-Hsi, and poured in one great mass over the whole of the densely-populated Honan, drowning millions of helpless people, and undoing the work of centuries. In a word, what the erratic river will do next is one of the chief problems of the physical future of China. It has already shifted its course no less than nine times in its troubled career; and on account of the great rapidity of its stream it is of little use for navigation. Could Yu have foreseen the destruction of all the grand works of which he boasted, he would probably have taken a less exalted view of what he had accomplished.

However that may be, his contemporaries were so impressed by his ability, and the great Chung so admired his virtue and talent, that he was chosen as heir in the life-time of that mighty sovereign. The dialogue said to have taken place between the Emperor and his subject on the question of the succession to the throne is curious and interesting:

"Come," said Chung to Yu, "I have been reigning for thirty-three years; my advanced age and growing infirmities prevent me from giving the necessary application to affairs of state. I wish you to reign instead. Do your utmost to acquit yourself worthily of the task."

"I am not virtuous enough to govern well," replied Yu; "the people will not obey me."

He then recommended some one else.

Chung, however, insisted in the following terms:

"When we had everything to fear from the great inundation, you worked with eagerness and rectitude; you rendered the greatest services, and your talents and wisdom were made manifest throughout the whole country. Although you have led an

FIG. 13.—A CHINESE BRIDGE SPANNING THE HOANG-HO.

unassuming life with your family, although you have served the State well, you have not considered that a reason to dispense with work, and this is no ordinary virtue. You have no pride; there is no one in the country superior to you in good qualities. None other has done such great things, and yet you do not set a high value on your own conduct. There is no one in the country whose merit excels your own."

So Yu became chief ruler, and his name was

associated by posterity with that of Yao and of Chung. The sacred book has preserved many of his sayings, and I will quote the most beautiful here:

"He who obeys reason is happy, he who resists it is unhappy. Virtue is the foundation of good government; the first task of government is to provide the people governed with all that is necessary for their subsistence and preservation. The next thing is to make the population virtuous; to teach them the proper use of everything; and lastly, to protect them from all which jeopardizes their health or their life. The prince who understands men well will appoint none to public offices but those who are wise; his generous heart and liberality will win him love."

When Yu died, the chiefs of the people unfortunately failed to carry on the custom of choosing as a successor to the throne the wisest and most illustrious of their number. The law of hereditary right was recognized, and dynasties henceforth succeeded each other in China as elsewhere, each lasting a long or short time according to whether the people were or were not satisfied. There was, however, one salutary exception to the usual interpretation of the hereditary principle. The reigning Emperor could choose as his successor the son he considered the most intelligent of his children; and as a Chinese ruler generally has at least fifty children, without counting the girls, there is no difficulty in making a selection.

CHAPTER II

Trip up the Shu-Kiang river—My fellow-passengers and their costumes—A damaged bell—Female peasants on the river-banks—I am caught up and carried off by a laughing virago—Arrival at Canton—Early trading between China and Ceylon and Africa, etc.—The Empress Lui-Tseu teaching the people to rear silk-worms—The treaties of Nanking and Tien-tsin—Bombardment of Canton—Murder of a French sailor and terrible revenge—M. Vaucher and I explore Canton—The *fêtes* in honour of the Divinity of the North and of the Queen of Heaven—General appearance of Canton—An emperor's recipe for making tea—How tea is grown in China—The Fatim garden—A dutiful son—Scene of the murder of the Tai-Ping rebels—The Temple of the five hundred Genii—Suicide of a young engineer—Return of his spirit in the form of a snake.

WELL-BUILT, comfortable steamers leave Hong-Kong daily for Canton. I embarked in one of them one fine spring morning, when a fresh sea-breeze was blowing, such as gives new life to those enervated by too long a residence in the tropics. I did not see a single white face amongst the passengers, for European trade is all transferred to Hong-Kong, now driven away from Canton by the burning by the Celestials of the fine factories built outside the gates of the city by European contractors.

My fellow-passengers, all Chinese, wore loose garments of blue cotton, thick-soled shoes, and a skull-cap, from which a long pig-tail, in many cases of false hair, hung down the back, reaching to the heels. The crew of American sailors as they navigated the vessel kept a watchful eye upon the passengers, for though the latter looked peaceable enough, there had been more than one instance of the sudden transformation of inoffensive travellers into daring pirates, who, after pillaging and burning the ship, had made for the nearest shore and escaped the vengeance of those they had robbed.

FIG. 14.—A PAGODA.

Before entering the great Shu-Kiang river, on the north bank of which Canton is built, we passed the ruins of a fort dating from the time of the Dutch supremacy. Beyond it the stream is bordered by green rice plantations with little hills

THE PEARL OF THE EAST

rising up here and there surmounted by isolated pagodas of several storeys high. On one of them I noticed standing out against the sky from the fifth storey the fragment of a bell, one-half of which had been shot away by a ball from a French cannon. Great indeed must have been the astonishment of the Chinese, posted on this particular pagoda to watch the movements of the enemies' troops, when the projectile struck the sonorous mass of bronze and shivered it to splinters. The catastrophe must have been to them a warning full of sinister yet salutary meaning.

The river rushes proudly along towards its final home in the ocean, but narrows before it reaches its actual mouth, the water becoming yellow, as does that of the Nile at the time of its rising. Even without glasses I could quite clearly make out several poor-looking villages, the houses with their dull red roofs occupied no doubt by fishermen and their families. Oh, how different were the surroundings of these water-highways of China to those of the Seine, the Rhone, and of the charming Gironde! How much I preferred even the Nile, which I had but recently left, to this so-called Pearl of the East, for in spite of the ugly black mud-huts of the fellaheen, there is something beautiful about the river-side scenery. I like the graceful date-tree far better than the bamboo with its self-conscious uprightness, and I considerably prefer the slim and supple Egyptian women to the clumsy, heavy-limbed female peasants of China, such as I saw on the banks of the Shu-

Kiang, dragging heavy loads behind them as they strode along in a manner which made me doubtful as to their sex, especially as their faces were hidden by the great hats they wore. A few more turns of the paddle-wheels of our steamer, and it stopped opposite Canton. In a moment a virago, such as those I had been looking at with anything but admiration, was on the deck, and seizing me in her strong arms as if I were a delicate baby, she quickly deposited me at the bottom of her own boat, roaring with laughter over my embarrassment. I had no longer any doubt as to her sex, as with a few vigorous strokes of her oars she ran her boat ashore, and with the same maternal care as she had shown before she landed me upon the wharf of the little island of Hainan where I was expected.

There is no particular historic interest attached to Canton except that it was the very first Chinese town to enter into relations with foreigners. We know that this opening of intercourse took place in the year 618 A.D., but whence the foreigners came is not so certain. Possibly some of them were from Ceylon, and undoubtedly others were from the continent of Africa, as proved by the fact that elephants' tusks, the horns of the rhinoceros, coral, pearls, redwood, and medicines were brought into the city by the strangers, who received metals in exchange—that is to say, copper, tin, and gold, and silk—especially silk—for it was manufactured in the Celestial Empire twenty-seven centuries before the Christian era. It was Lui-Tseu, the wife of the great Emperor Kwang-Ti, or the Yellow ruler, who taught the people the art of rearing the silk-worm and spinning the material it produced. The industry of silk-weaving has brought such wealth to China that Lui-Tseu has been raised to the rank of a beneficent genius, and is honoured under the name of the "Spirit of the mulberry-tree and the silk-worm."

In 1127 an edict was issued forbidding the exportation of metal, and ordering all payments to be made from henceforth in money alone. It is recorded in Chinese annals that at a considerably later date a French vessel came up the river Shu-Kiang and fired her cannons in an aggressive manner, so that relations with foreigners were broken off.

In 1425, however, an embassy from Portugal resulted in the re-admission of foreigners to Canton, and a century later the Dutch also obtained a footing in the city.

They in their turn were, however, supplanted by the English, who practically enjoyed a monopoly of trade from the beginning of the eighteenth century until 1834. At that date their prosperity began to decline, one dispute succeeding another, and in 1839 open war broke out between England and China. In 1841 Hong-Kong was ceded to the former power, and in 1842 the Treaty of Nanking was signed, opening to British traders the five ports of Canton, Amoy, Fuchau, Ningpo, and Shanghai. Fresh friction was caused by the arrogant assumptions of the Chinese and the vacillating policy of the English, culminating in the war of 1856, the immediate cause of which was the capture by the Chinese of a lorcha, or small hybrid vessel of European build, with the rigging of a Chinese junk flying the British flag. After a fierce struggle a peace was again patched up, but the factories outside Canton had all been destroyed by the mob, and prosperity has never since fully returned to the city. It was not until 1860, when the Convention of Pekin was signed, ratifying the Treaty of Tientsin, that anything like cordial relations were established between England and China, and since then these relations have been again and again disturbed.

Before the bombardment of Canton by the united fleets of England and France every foreigner found within the walls of that inhospitable town was beheaded at once. Naturally, with the memory of all that had so recently happened fresh in my mind, I hesitated when M. Vaucher, representative on the island of Hainan, of the Swiss house of the same name, suggested that we should go together through the streets of Canton in sedan chairs. I did not like to allude to the danger I might run myself, but I asked if I should not be exposing him to peril. "No," was his reply, "your fellow-countrymen have won the permanent respect of the people for all foreigners, and you will be able to boast on your return home of having explored the vast city with no other protector than myself."

A TERRIBLE REVENGE

M. Vaucher then told me the following story:

"After the allied fleets had taken possession of Canton, the commanders used to send a party of men every morning to get fresh fruit for the table of the officers, and rarely did a day pass without at least one Englishman being absent at calling over. Any sailor, who to satisfy his curiosity was foolish enough to leave his comrades for a moment, was at once set upon by Chinese soldiers and murdered in the open street. Vainly did the Admiral of the English fleet threaten to make bloody reprisals if the authorities did not punish the offenders. The same kind of thing happened again and again. At last one day five or six sailors belonging to a French frigate landed and made their way into Canton. As they turned into a street they missed one of their party, and presently they found his headless corpse lying on the ground. When the crime became known to the French, the second in command of the fleet collected fifty volunteers, armed them with revolvers and hatchets, and landing with them, marched them into Canton. On arriving in the street where the murder had been committed, some of the men were told off to guard the entrances to it, whilst the rest made their way into the houses and killed all the Chinese they found in them except one, who, though he had already been hit by six bullets, calmly walked up the middle of the street without quickening his pace or even turning his head to the right or the left at the sound of the renewed firing. The leader of the expedition at last ran up to him and gave him a smart blow on the shoulder. The fearless Celestial merely turned his pale face towards his

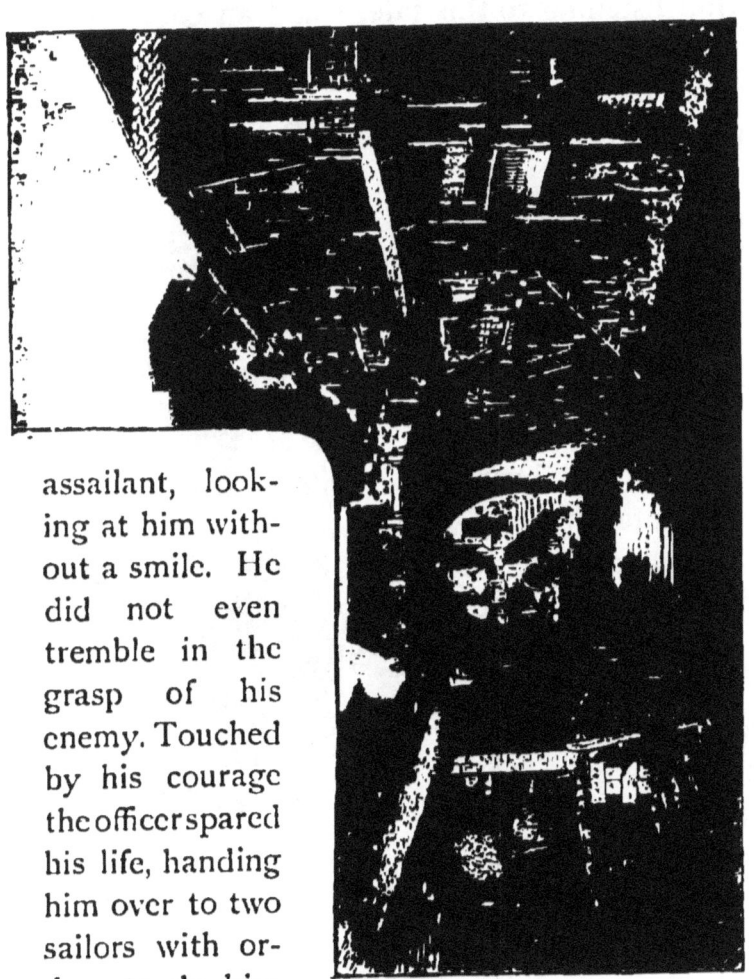

FIG. 15.—A STREET IN CANTON.

assailant, looking at him without a smile. He did not even tremble in the grasp of his enemy. Touched by his courage the officer spared his life, handing him over to two sailors with orders to do him no harm.

"After this bloody punishment, which was very hostilely criticized by the English press of Hong-Kong and Shanghai, Europeans, whatever their

I EXPLORE CANTON

nationality, have been able to wander about unmolested either alone or in parties in the streets of Canton."

After listening to this tale, I had an eager desire to explore the town, which, since the departure of the allied fleets, had rarely been entered by Europeans. I watched anxiously for the first symptom in the faces of the inhabitants of the hereditary hatred of white men, which had most likely been greatly intensified by the bombardment of the town, and by the punishment inflicted for the murder of the French sailors, a punishment by no means excessive, terrible as it was. I am bound to add, however, that as M. Vaucher and I

FIG. 16.—A WOMAN OF THE PEOPLE WITH HER BABY.

were carried rapidly through the crowded streets by our coolies, in our respective chairs, we noted no hostility in the placid faces of those we encountered. The people stood aside to let us pass, and showed rather benevolent curiosity than insulting indifference. The Chinese children, with their round heads and strongly-marked eyebrows, who are so aggressive and impudent in the interior of the country, here remained perfectly silent. Only the old women tottering along on their deformed feet paused in their painful walk now and then, to lean against the walls of the houses, and look at us in a mocking though not exactly a hostile manner. Our progress was only once arrested for a moment, when we met a great military mandarin in a narrow street, escorted by some ten warriors bearing their halberds on their shoulders. The mandarin stopped, and we passed without difficulty, giving him a military salute in return for his courtesy.

FIG. 17.—A CHINESE MANDARIN.

I confess that this unexpected complaisance put me into a very good humour, and after this incident I gave myself up without reserve to the enjoyment of my first visit to a Chinese town.

By a lucky chance I had arrived at the very moment when the inhabitants were celebrating two of their greatest festivals. The first, in honour of the beautiful Paktai, the fair Divinity of the North, was simply remarkable for the immense crowds flocking to the pagodas, crowds made up of bonzes, bonzesses, portly mandarins, cooks and barbers vigorously plying their trades, æsthetes with effeminate faces, young girls full of delight at getting out of their palanquins for once, and at being able to totter about on the flag-stones of the temples for a few minutes on their poor mutilated feet.

When the gilded pedestal upholding the shrine of Paktai was completely hidden beneath the flowers flung upon it by the crowds, the worshippers all repaired *en masse* to see the theatrical representations which take place after the religious ceremony. Not until midnight did every one go home, only to meet again the next day, when a great procession passed through the city, in the midst of which the venerated idol was carried with the greatest pomp. Some on horseback, others in sedan chairs, were many young boys and girls wearing the costumes in vogue amongst the heroes and heroines of the earliest days of the Celestial Empire. Many too were the banners of beautiful

FIG. 18.—A GONG-RINGER.

silk embroidered with various devices or inscriptions in golden letters, and still more numerous were the bearers of the large gongs, some of which were of such an immense circumference that it took two strong coolies to carry them.

All Asiatics love a deafening noise, and the delight of the Chinese may be imagined when the accumulated din of these great bronze disks becomes one continuous roar like thunder.

The second *fête* I witnessed was celebrated in the Honam suburb in honour of Tien-Ho, the Queen of Heaven, and the protectress of sailors. All the ship-owners of the populous city of Canton, all the pilots, all the captains of junks and sampans, all the fishermen, boatmen, and boatwomen,

FIG. 19.—A CHINESE ACTOR.

A GRAND DRAMA

—in fact, every human creature connected in the remotest degree with anything like shipping or boats, were collected in front of the sanctuary of the goddess. Her statue too was covered with flowers, and, as in the case of the *fête* of the Divinity of the North, the theatre opened directly the pagoda of the Queen of Heaven closed. The stage was erected about a hundred yards from the pagoda, so that the devout had only to turn round to pass at once from the sacred to the profane.

A grand spectacular drama, called the Marriage of the Ocean and the Earth, extended over twelve consecutive evenings; the only plot was, however, the presentation to each other by the betrothed couple of the vast treasures at their disposal.

The Earth began by a grand show of tigers, lions, elephants, ostriches, etc.—in a word, of all the big animals which our ancestor Noah took with him into the ark. Then the Ocean, not to be outdone, paraded in his turn his dolphins, his turtles, the vessels he had engulfed, his corals, and great bunches of all the most wonderful growths of his submarine gardens. All these marvels were, however, nothing but a prelude to the great final surprise, when an enormous whale reeled into view, and as it flopped about shot out a great volume of water over the whole stage. It would be impossible to describe the enthusiastic delight of the spectators, who all shouted like madmen, *Has! Hung haho!* (excellent! perfect!) and if M.

Vaucher and I had not applauded too we should have been stoned.

The beautiful river on which Canton is built presented for many days a most picturesque appearance. I could wish those of my readers who love the marvellous, who enjoy looking at crowds and do not mind noise, no better pleasure than to gaze, if but for a moment, upon the Pearl of the East at this *fête* of the protectress of those who do their business on the great waters, thronged as its surface then is with junks dressed with flags, brilliantly illuminated flower-boats, little vessels transformed for the nonce into miniature pagodas, gliding mysteriously along as do the gondolas of Venice. I was told that on these occasions more than one lovely young Celestial maiden is worshipped in these pagodas of a day, with a ritual very different from that of the public ceremony we had witnessed at the shrine of the goddess.

Canton consists of a great number of narrow streets, each house in which is adorned with coloured signs, giving a very quaint and charming appearance to the façades, especially of an evening, when the gilt lettering on the red and black lacquer ground is lit up by the rays of the setting sun. As was the case in European towns in mediæval times, and is still customary in the Orient, each district of the city has its own special industry, and is closed at nightfall by a bamboo barrier. The cobblers' quarter seemed to me to be the most densely populated; a great multitude of workers, naked to the waist, zealously plying their trade, chattering like magpies the while. Close to the cobblers live the coffin-makers, who are even noisier than their neighbours, and quite as happy over their work. Yet another quarter dear to the lovers of *bric-à-brac*, is sacred to the manufacture of porcelain, bronzes, cloisonné enamels, beautifully lacquered or delicately carved boxes in ebony, ivory, and other materials, plain and figured silks, etc., which are sent to Hong-Kong for trans-shipment to Europe and America.

You can of course get all these things without going all the way to China for them, and they are to be seen in Paris in the Guimet and Cernuschi Museums, and at various Oriental houses in London and New York. Many Chinese are very wealthy, and keep for themselves and their heirs the art treasures they buy or have inherited from their ancestors.

In spite of the fact that you can see Chinese curios at home, it would be a pity to miss the

FIG. 20.—A CHINESE ACTOR IN A TRAGIC PART.

pleasure of rummaging in the shops. The owner of those you enter will receive you with apparent cordiality, but at the same time with a certain distrustful politeness, and you will be carefully watched as you turn over the goods for sale. If you accept the cup of tea which every merchant delights to offer to his visitors, and you seem to appreciate the superior quality of the beverage, you will win the golden opinion of the donor, for to the Celestial tea is a divine plant. The drink made from it as a matter of fact quenches thirst better than any other, not only in the heat of summer, but also in the extreme cold of the heights of the Himalayas or of the desert of Gobi, where the traveller is exposed to the icy blast of the north wind. From the east to the west, from the north to the south of the vast Empire, we meet with the hospitable tea-house; it is perhaps not quite such a fascinating place as it is in Japan, but beneath its shelter the traveller is always sure of finding the cheering beverage which will put new strength into him for his further journey. There is not a Chinese poet who has failed to sing the praises of the precious shrub. Even an illustrious Emperor wrote directions in verse (reproduced below in dull prose) for the preparation of a cup of tea, and described the salutary effect it has upon the mind :

"Put a tripod pot, the colour and form of which testifies to long service, upon a moderate fire; fill this pot with the pure water of melted snow, and heat this water to the degree

AN IMPERIAL TEA-MAKER

needed for turning fish white or crabs red, and then pour it at once into a cup containing the tender leaves of a choice tea; leave it to simmer until the steam, which will at first rise up copiously, forms thick clouds which gradually disperse, till all that is left is a light mist upon the surface; then sip the delicious liquor slowly; it will effectually dissipate all the causes for anxiety which are worrying you. You can taste, you can feel the peaceful bliss which results from imbibing the liquid thus prepared, but it is perfectly impossible to describe it. Already, however, I hear the ringing of the curfew-bell; the freshness of the night is increasing; the moonbeams penetrate through the slits in my tent, and light up the few pieces of furniture adorning it. I am without anxiety and without fatigue, my digestion is perfect; I can give myself to repose without fear. These verses were written to the best of my small ability, in the spring of the tenth month of the year Ping-yn (1746) of my reign.

(Signed) KHIAN-LUNG."

The tea-plant is a shrub requiring very little care. A siliceous soil suits it best, and in it it attains its fullest development. Great quantities of seed are sown in September and October, and when the plants are about nine inches high they are transplanted and placed about twenty inches apart. When the leaves have reached their fullest development they are gathered, carefully washed to remove any earth which may have clung to them, and they are then exposed to the rays of the sun, the day chosen for this part of the preparation being the very hottest in the year. In the evening the dry leaves are taken up with every precaution against injury, placed in boxes, and protected from the air by sheets of lead. Millions of cases of tea thus packed are dispersed all over the world, but it is needless to add that the Chinese keep the best leaves for their own consumption. Green, or as they themselves call it, white tea, is put into boxes directly it is picked, without any drying or other preparation, and black tea is produced by placing the leaves in a brazier over a slow fire, these leaves being constantly turned over with the hands by the men in charge of them, to prevent them from sticking together or drying too quickly. When taken from the brazier they are placed in a sieve and still further manipulated, always with the greatest care and delicacy. Lastly, they are once more exposed to heat in the brazier to give them the brown colour so much esteemed by many consumers. It is in this last stage of the preparation that the skill of the manipulator is put to the severest test, for if the tea is too much burnt it will have no taste at all, and if it is not sufficiently burnt it will be bitter and heating.

I forget now in whose house it was, but I was on one occasion stupid enough, when the guest of a mandarin, to say I had once at the residence of a clergyman drunk an excellent cup of tea mixed with rum and sweetened with sugar.

"Sugar and rum!" cried my host, who was terribly shocked. "We must take care not to offer our best teas to you, for you would certainly not be able to appreciate them."

I stopped eight days at Canton; more than enough to visit everything worth seeing in that now uninteresting city. I saw the endless rice-fields stretching away beyond its gates; I went to look at the French concession, where there is not a single French inhabitant, though the names of the streets, such as the *Rue de la Fusée*, the *Rue de la Dordogne*, and the *Rue de la Charente*, recall the

FIG. 21.—A VILLA NEAR CANTON.

vessels once manned by the brave sailors who had for a brief time sojourned in this remote Chinese town. One curiosity which every visitor to Canton ought to see, is the so-called Fatim garden, where each tree represents some fantastic animal, and in which prowl herds of pigs, more quaint in appearance than the shrubs tended by pale-faced young bonzes wearing yellow garments.

The cemetery of Canton is of vast extent, and every year in the month of May, the pious Celestials all flock to it in white robes, to lay offerings of rice, fruit, and flowers on the graves of those they have lost. The gifts would be left unmolested for a long time, but for the fact that they are presented in the spring, just when countless birds are nesting in the branches of the lofty bamboos growing in the neighbourhood, and who consequently look upon the rice and fruit as provided especially for them.

It is not only after the death of those near and dear to them, that the Chinese show the deep filial love for their parents which is one of their most striking characteristics. The *Pekin Gazette* gave a very touching instance of this reverent affection, communicated to the official organ of the Celestial Empire by the Governor of Schantung, which made such a sensation that it reached the ears of the Emperor himself. Here is the story:

A certain native of China, Li-Hsien-Ju by name, whose father had died at Feï-Chang, immediately sold the piece of land he inherited in order to give a grand funeral in honour of his beloved and lamented father. The time of mourning had not yet expired when a terrible famine took place in the town where the ceremonies were going on. Provisions became so scarce and so dear, that Li-Hsien-Ju found himself quite unable to provide properly for his aged mother, so he decided to carry her on his back to another province where the ground was less sterile. This he did, begging his way as he went, and supporting himself and his sacred charge on alms alone.

. This model son, laden as he was, actually traversed the fabulous distance of four hundred French leagues, finally arriving at Honan, where he and his mother settled down. A year after this the poor mother was taken ill, and Li-Hsien-Ju, fearing that she might die in a strange land, of which every Chinese has the greatest horror, resolved to take her home to her native country in the same manner as he had brought her from it, so he started back again with his sacred burden, begging his way once more. The two got back again to Feï-Chang at last, but had scarcely reached their home before the old mother died. It is impossible to tell how many nights the heart-broken son spent on the tomb of the lost one, but we know that, thanks to his pious efforts, the bones of his father were laid beside the body of his mother. A few days after the death of the latter, the grief of the orphan became so terrible that he wept tears of blood. He is now sixty years old, but he still mourns for his parents, and in the month of May when the *fête* of the dead is held, he never fails to drag himself to the cemetery and place upon the tomb, according to custom, a bowl of smoking rice of gleaming whiteness.

There are no Monthyon prizes, such as those given by the French Academy for acts of disinterested goodness, or surely this unselfish son would have received one.

M. Vaucher and I went to visit the quay outside Canton, which was the scene of the massacre of 100,000 Tai-Ping rebels, after the defeat of Hung-Hsiu-ch'wan in 1865. The ferocious mandarin Yeh had them all decapitated at the edge of the river Kwan-Tung, their heads falling into the muddy stream. A Dutchman, who had belonged to a factory in Canton at the time, told me that he witnessed the terrible scene from his window, and had been greatly struck by the extraordinary composure with which the victims met their fate. Motionless and with bowed heads they knelt at the edge of the quay, awaiting the fatal stroke of the sword. " I had some idea," added the Dutchman, "of sending the poor fellows some packets of cigarettes to cheer their last moments, but I should have been completely ruined, for their numbers increased every day."

The tragic story of the Tai-Ping rebellion, its extraordinary success at first, and its final suppression under Gordon is well known. In the two campaigns against the Tai-Pings, the future hero of Khartoum fought no less than thirty-three battles, besieging and taking numerous walled cities, and changing the whole history of the vast Celestial Empire. Had the revolt been finally successful, as it at one time bid fair to be, Hung, the enlightened leader, might have founded a new dynasty, and warded off for a long time at least the dismemberment of the once vast Empire of the East.

My last visit was to the so-called Temple of the five hundred genii, containing five hundred grotesque gilded statues, taller than life, and of a surprising girth. We must not, however, make fun of them, for each one represents some Celestial who has made his mark in art, science, or philosophy. In France such a temple would be called a Pantheon, and that is what it really is, a place set apart for the commemoration of the great ones of the past.

In the Temple of the five hundred genii lived a beautiful little water-snake, which a bonze of venerable appearance tended with reverent care, feeding it on green frogs and cantharides. I tried to find out why he set such store upon it, and the following story was told to me:

The river, from the banks of which rises the great city of Canton, often overflows, and the inundations caused by the excess of water do a great deal of mischief to the rice plantations. A young engineer was ordered to construct an embankment, but he must have done his work badly, for only a year after its completion the river again burst its bounds, and the engineer in despair drowned himself in the waters he had failed to control. Yet another inundation took place after his death, and in the mud cast up by it upon the shore was found a little snake. By order of the Viceroy the reptile was taken to the Temple of the five hundred genii, and a miracle at once took place, for it had no sooner entered the sacred precincts than the waters subsided. Every one attributed their fall to gratitude for the kind welcome given to the little snake, and a long memorial on the subject was addressed by the Viceroy to the Emperor, which was at once published by the *Pekin Gazette*. An explanation of the phenomenon was added, to the effect that the little snake was really none other than the engineer who had committed suicide. There was really nothing surprising in the matter, for of course by his death the unfortunate young man had become a Chen-Ching-tung-Chang-chan, or divinity of the river, and was anxious to repair the mistake made in his lifetime on earth, by exercising a benevolent influence over its waters now that he had the power to do so.

After the miracle which had taken place on the entrance into the Temple of the little snake, the people had proclaimed it to be the genius of the water, and as such they venerated and cherished it!

CHAPTER III

General Tcheng-Ki-Tong and his book on China—The monuments of China—Those the Chinese delight to honour—A Chinese heroine—Ingredients of the "Cup of Immortality"—Avenues of colossal statues and monsters in cemeteries—Imperial edict in honour of K'wo-Fan—Proclamation of the eighteenth century—The Emperor takes his people's sins upon himself—Reasons for Chinese indifference to matters of faith—Lao-Tsze, or the old philosopher—His early life—His book, the *Tao-Teh-King*—His theory of the creation—Affinity of his doctrine with Christianity—Quotations from his book.

GENERAL TCHENG-KI-TONG, who lived so long in France and married a French lady, although rumour says he already had a wife in China, wrote a very interesting but far from exhaustive book, with the title, *The Chinese described by themselves.* He said nothing in it of the worship of great men and of certain animals in his native land, nor did he refer to the way in which acts of virtue and of courage are rewarded there.

I will now endeavour to supplement the information given us by the learned general. In addition to the statues erected in China, as in the chief cities of Europe, to every man who has in any way distinguished himself, triumphal arches are set up in memory of those who have done heroic deeds, whether in the privacy of home life or in public. These arches are known as *Pai-lans*, or Honorary Portals, and as a rule they have three arcades, sometimes made of very fine stone worked with considerable skill, and surmounted by a roof of varnished canvas with the corners gracefully turned upwards as is the fashion in China. There are two kinds of monuments in the Celestial Empire, one of very ornate, the other of simple construction.

FIG. 22.—GENERAL TCHENG-KI-TONG.

Widows who refuse to marry again; virgins who have kept their vows of chastity till their death; men who have distinguished themselves in science, literature, or philosophy; diplomatists who by their skill in deception have mystified their colleagues as well as foreign ministers, and thus won a reputation for great wisdom; soldiers who have fought valiantly for their country; women who have committed suicide after a lost battle; wealthy men who have given much away in charity; families who have lived for many generations in one house; old men who can assemble in the home of their ancestors four living and healthy representatives of four generations, are honoured by the erection of Honorary Portals, which are also set up in general commemoration of any victory or series of victories in war.

In the centre of the larger and grander monuments are inscribed three words, signifying Faith, Submission, and Justice.

The Imperial Government of China goes out of its way to honour certain acts of abstinence, such as the refusal of a widow to marry again, erecting a monument to her when she has been true to her resolve till she is fifty years old, and has lived alone for at least twenty years. I must add that the Emperor himself contributes forty piastres, or about eight English pounds, to the expense of erecting monuments in honour of women who have been true to the memory of their husbands; he also gives a roll of silk to each inconsolable widow, and what is more, he has written a poem on widowhood. Who shall say after all this that the Chinese are not jealous of marital faithfulness? Monuments to widows are more imposing than any others, and bear an inscription signifying Chastity and Purity.

An affianced couple, who, though engaged in early childhood, have been prevented through some local rebellion, or through a foreign war, from accomplishing their union before they are fifty years old, are honoured in a similar manner.

A monument with the inscription "Chastity and Filial Piety" may be erected to glorify a Chinese mother, who having borne one child, takes a vow never to have another, in order to be free to devote herself to the needs of her poor parents. Similar honour may be done to young boys or girls who allow a piece of flesh to be taken from their arms or thighs, under the belief that this flesh mixed with certain ingredients will do their suffering parents good. The Imperial Government both approves and rewards the bloody sacrifice, the motive of which is that filial love held in such high esteem throughout the whole Celestial Empire.

On certain monuments with three arcades an inscription may be read, signifying, "Joy and Gladness to the Benevolent." Monuments such as these are erected in honour of some Chinese who has brought up orphans as if they were his own children, or of some rich man who has given a large sum of money towards the making of roads or bridges. A kind-hearted employer who pays poor men for collecting the bones scattered about the cemeteries and giving them reverent burial, is also often rewarded by the erection of a monument to his memory.

Those of the Celestials who distinguish themselves by charity, but who do not spend large sums of money, receive tablets of wood, on which are inscribed pious sentences composed by the Son of Heaven, that is to say, the Emperor. Many of these tablets, which answer the same purpose as did the Greek *stelæ*, are to be seen in the rooms known as the Halls of the Ancestors in the houses of the Chinese, especially those of the wealthy mandarins. They constitute regular patents of nobility, and are not won by favour or intrigue, as are so many titles in Europe, but by real acts of charity performed by their owners.

Three brothers, who have all passed their eightieth year and are still in good health, can have a monument erected announcing this fact, and so can husbands or wives who attain the age of one hundred.

At Amoy, in the province of Pecheli, are two monuments with arcades erected to the memory of the Chinese women who flung themselves into the wells of their houses when they heard the shouts of the English soldiers and sailors entering the town.

This act of despair is explained by the fact that the Chinese themselves give no quarter when they enter any place as victors; the men are strangled, and the women become the slaves of those who take them prisoners. In the very centre of Canton is a temple remarkable alike for its size and beauty. It was built in honour of the memory of a great Chinese lady, who in December 1857 committed suicide when the English and French took the city. This heroine, the wife of Pun-Yu, one of the chief magistrates at Canton, learning that the allies already occupied the northern portion of the town, put on her most magnificent apparel, and summoning all her servants, gave to each a parting present. She then killed herself by drinking what the bonzes call the "cup of immortality," a very strong poison, containing amongst other ingredients opium and the droppings of peacocks. This potent poison has often been given to emperors under pretext of making them immortal, but really with a view to getting rid of them.

There is yet another mode of honouring the illustrious departed. The children of civil and military officers have the right of erecting avenues of colossal figures opposite the tombs of their parents; these figures representing giants or monsters. The length of the avenues and the size of the figures is regulated by law, according to the grade of those they are intended to honour. The state itself pays for these quaint memorials, unless the necessary sum has been raised by voluntary subscriptions.

On the death of any illustrious soldier or politician whose firmness has added to the stability of the throne, the Emperor always hastens to give publicity to his grief at the public loss, and his gratitude for the services rendered by the deceased. Here is a specimen of an Imperial proclamation such as is frequently issued:

IMPERIAL EDICT.

"The deceased K'wo-Fan was a man of great knowledge, of varied talent, of profound penetration, of stainless morality, and of incorruptible honesty. He left the schools with the title of doctor; his merits were discovered by the Emperor Tao-K'an, who promoted him to the rank of Chingerh (colonel).

"In the reign of Hsien-Feng, he was commissioned to raise an army in Hunan, and after the battles in which he was victorious over the Tai-Ping rebels, he received the praises of the Emperor and the thanks of the whole country. It was then that my predecessor appointed him to the viceroyalty of the two Kiangs, and named him Generalissimo of the Imperial forces. During my own reign I made him chief Secretary of State. He became to me a second self; he was my life, my heart, and my backbone. I therefore bestowed on him the title of hereditary count, and I authorized him to wear the double peacock's feather. I had hoped that he would live long for me to heap fresh favours upon him, so that the news of his death has filled me with sorrow and dismay. I wish that according to custom three thousand taëls[1] should be spent on his funeral. A jarful of wine shall also be poured out on his tomb by General Mutengah, chief of the Manchu garrison at Nanking. Two tablets of stone, bearing his name, shall be erected, one at Nanking in the Temple of the Loyal and the Illustrious, the other in Pekin in the Pantheon of the Wise and Good.

"I wish the life of K'wo-Fan to be written and given into the care of the Imperial historiographers, that the memory of a life so beautiful may be preserved in the national annals. His son will inherit the title of count, and I give him dispensation from an audience.

"I appoint Ho-Ching, lieutenant-general of Kiang-Su, to be instructor of the children and grand-children of the deceased. A token of my munificence will be given to them, that they may know how my throne remembers and honours a loyal servant.

"Let this edict be respected!"

The homage rendered to heroes, wise men, and

[1] A taël is worth about five shillings.

philanthropists, has its origin in the religious principles inculcated by Chinese philosophers. These philosophers were very numerous in China in past days, and it is only possible to give an account here of the most celebrated of them.

Some twenty-three centuries before the Christian era the Chinese simply worshipped one Supreme Being, first under the vague name of Thian, or Heaven; later under the more personal title of Ti Shang, or the Great One.

Gradually, however, this monotheism was succeeded by the deification of the heavenly bodies, each with a priest of its own, whose business it was to advise those responsible for the government of China. These priests, who became in course of time extremely powerful, won their influence through the study of astronomy; but as that influence sometimes ran counter to the wishes of the emperors and bid fair to supersede their power, they eventually suppressed the entire hierarchy. In Europe this interference with the spiritual guides of the people would have aroused a passion of fanaticism, and have resulted in massacres and religious wars, but nothing of the kind occurred in China, for there the martyr's palm and crown are never coveted, and religious zeal never produces the terrible results with which the student of European history is familiar. Truly, the Celestials are to be congratulated on the calmness with which they accept what they consider the inevitable.

The following characteristic epitome of the

religious ideas in vogue amongst the Chinese in
B.C. 1760, is taken from a proclamation issued
to his people by the Emperor then on the
throne:

"Shang-Ti, the supreme ruler, has given reason
to man, and if he listens to its dictates his spirit
will exist for ever, but if he does not he will revert
to nothingness."

"The ruler of Hia," continues this old-world
proclamation, "extinguished in his soul the light
of reason, and inflicted a thousand ills upon the
people in all the States of the Empire. Oppressed
and unable longer to endure such tyranny, the
people made known to the spirits of high and low
degree, that they were unjustly dealt with. The
eternal reason of Heaven gives happiness to the
virtuous, and misery to the vicious and depraved,
and this is why Heaven has visited Hia with all
manner of calamities to make his crimes manifest
to all.

"As a result of this, all unworthy though I be, I
have felt it my duty to conform to the unmistakable and terrible decrees of Heaven. I dared not
leave such great crimes unpunished, but I did dare
to take a black bullock to serve as the sacrifice I
felt bound to offer. I ventured to appeal to the
august Heaven and to the divine ruler of the earth.
. . . To each of you I have assigned the States he
is to govern. Beware of obeying unjust laws or
adopting unjust customs. Do not fall into the
mistakes which result from idleness, nor yield to

love of pleasure. By observing and obeying wise and equitable laws, you will be following the commands of Heaven. . . . All is sifted in the heart of Shang-Ti. The crimes any or all of you commit will be visited on me alone, but if I do evil you will have no part in it."

In this quaint address is shadowed forth the beautiful idea that the Emperor is responsible to God for his people, though they are not responsible for him. A similar thought is apparent in the following quotation from a kind of penitential psalm which the same Emperor is said to have composed on the occasion of a famine which decimated China during his reign. Feeling that he must have done something to arouse the wrath of Heaven, he cut off the long hair and nails which are the special pride of highly-born Celestials, and laying aside his Imperial robes, wrapped himself in the skins of beasts. Thus disguised he went forth alone to a mountain and vented his grief and remorse for having :

1. Neglected to instruct his subjects as he ought to have done.

2. For failing to win them back to their duty when they had departed from it.

3. For having built grand palaces, and incurred other expenses by unnecessary building.

4. For having too many wives, and loving them too much.

5. For caring too much for the delicacies of the table.

FIG. 23.—LAO-TSZE.
(*Univers l'ittoresque.*)

6. And lastly, for having lent too ready an ear to the flattery of his favourites, and of certain high officials of his court.

Another significant and noteworthy fact brought out alike in the proclamation and confession of this enlightened ruler is, that there is no idea of any intermediary being necessary between him and God. It is the same to this day, no priest intervenes between the Emperor and Shang-Ti, and the bonzes who spend their lives studying the moral precepts of Lao-Tsze and Confucius are merely thinkers who never interfere in affairs of State or with the religious teaching of the people. Hence the total indifference of the Chinese to matters of faith; they believe in free-will, and act in accordance with that belief.

In the sixth and seventh centuries before our era the Chinese Empire was in a condition little short of anarchy. The wealthy were depraved, the poor were steeped in misery, and everywhere injustice and oppression were the rule. The emperors frittered away their lives in their harems, giving no thought to the welfare of their people. It was time indeed for a reformer to arise, and the first to appear was the great Lao-Tsze, who is supposed to have been born about 604 B.C., fifty years before the yet greater Kung-Fu-tze, or, as he is called by Europeans, Confucius.

The state of the Celestial Empire when Lao-Tsze first began to inculcate his peculiar doctrines was corrupt in the extreme, greatly resembling that of the Roman Empire in the time of Nero, when the disciples of Christ preached equality and contempt for riches, striving to win souls from the awful depravity and sensuality of the heathen world, and to teach them to aspire to an ideal and divine love and to the immaterial joys of the Christian heaven. Lao-Tsze, who was to inaugurate the great reform completed later by Confucius, began his public career as curator of the library of the King of the Tcheou, in what was then the city of Lob, not far from that of Lob-yang in the present province of Honan. His real name is supposed to have been Erh-Li, but that of Lao-Tsze, signifying the old philosopher, has entirely superseded it. Whilst keeper of the royal books he is said to have read many of the works of Indian philosophers, and from them to have imbibed the principles embodied in his own immortal work, called the *Tao-Teh-King*, the exact meaning of the title of which has been so much discussed, but is generally translated the "Book of Supreme reason and virtue." If, as may well be, the word *Tao* is identical with the Greek Θεος and with the Latin *Deus*, both of which mean God, then the proper rendering of *Tao-Teh-King* is the "Book of God and of reason." However that may be, it is certain that its author was a true theist, rightly considered the founder of Theism, which is one of the three doctrines held in equal honour by the Celestials, the other two being Confucianism and Buddhism.

Many legends have gathered about the memory of Lao-Tsze, and the young Confucius is said to have met the old philosopher more than once. The former is reported to have said after an interview in Pekin with his forerunner: "To-day I have seen Lao-Tsze, and can only liken him to a dragon who mounts aloft in the clouds, I cannot tell how, and rises to heaven." Another story is that the older Chinese philosopher travelled in India and there met Pythagoras, the great mathematician and believer in the transmigration of souls; but if so, there is no trace of the influence of the Greek in the *Tao-Teh-King*, which must have been written before its author left China. As a matter of fact, very little is really known of the life of Lao-Tsze, but some idea of his peculiar views can be obtained from the following quotations from his book:

"God," he says, "is spiritual and material, so that He has two kinds of existence. We emanate in the first instance from the former or spiritual nature, to enter later into the second. Our aim upon earth should be to return to the first, or spiritual nature. To succeed in this we must refrain from the pleasures of the world, control our passions, and practise boundless charity."

It is the advocacy of this boundless charity which justifies us in comparing the doctrine of Lao-Tsze with primitive Christianity. Before, however, we give proofs of this affinity it will be interesting to note how the old philosopher proves his assertion, that all the material forms of nature are but emanations from the divine.

In the twenty-fifth section of the *Tao-Teh-King* we read :

"Beings of corporeal form were made from matter which was at first in a chaotic condition.

"Before the heaven and the earth came into being, there was nothing but a profound silence, a boundless void, without any perceptible form.

"It[1] existed alone, infinite, immutable.

"It moved about in the illimitable space without undergoing any change.

"It may be looked upon as the mother of the Universe.

"I am ignorant of its name, but I call it the Tao, by which I mean supreme and universal Reason.

"Constrained to make a name for it, I designate it by its attributes, and call it grand, lofty.

"Having recognized that it is grand and lofty, I add that it is all-embracing.

"Having recognized that it is infinite, I designate it as unlike myself. . . .

"The earth is ruled by Heaven.

"Heaven is ruled by the Tao or universal Reason.

"Universal Reason is a law unto itself."

These quotations cannot fail to give an exalted idea of the principles advocated by the Chinese sage. They even shadow forth, to some extent, the doctrine of the Gospel, which was not preached until 600 years after the death of the author of the *Tao-Teh-King;* but the extract I give now

---

[1] Lao-Tsze speaks of the Supreme Being as "it," not "he," and implies that his Tao, whatever he signified by it, may have existed even before God.—TRANS.

from the forty-ninth section of the book on Supreme Reason is yet more strikingly significant:

"The heart of a holy man is not inexorable.

"His heart is in sympathy with the hearts of all other men.

"A virtuous man should be treated according to his virtue.

"A vicious man should be treated as if he also were virtuous. Herein is wisdom and virtue."

Again in the sixteenth section we read:

"To be just, and equitable to all, is to have the attributes of God.

"Having the attributes of God is to be of the divine nature.

"To be of the divine nature is to succeed in becoming identified with the Tao or the supreme and universal Reason.

"To be identified with the supreme Reason is to win eternal life.

"Even when the body is put to death, there is no need to have any fear of annihilation."

So much for Lao-Tsze's belief in the immortality of the soul; now note in what touching terms he expresses his compassion for the unhappy and unfortunate:

"If the people suffer from hunger, it is because they are weighed down by taxes too heavy for them.

"This is the cause of their misery. . . .

"If the people are difficult to govern, it is because they are oppressed by work too hard for them. . . .

"This is the cause of their insubordination.

"If the people are indifferent to the approach of death, it is because they find it too difficult to obtain sufficient nourishment.

"That is why they die with so little regret."

CHAPTER IV

Lao-Tsze and Confucius compared—The appearance of Kilin, the fabulous dragon, to the father of Confucius—Early life of the Philosopher—The death and funeral of his mother—His views on funeral ceremonies—His visit to the King of Lu and discourse on the nature of man—Confucius advocates gymnasium exercises—His love of music—His summary of the whole duty of woman—He describes the life of a widow—He gives a list of the classes of men to be avoided in marriage—The seven legitimate reasons for the divorce of a wife—The three exceptions rendering divorce illegal—The missionary Gutzlaff's opinion of Confucius' view of woman's position—The Philosopher meets a man about to commit suicide—He rescues him from despair—He loses thirteen of his own followers.

UNDER the continued influence of Lao-Tsze, China would probably have become in course of time crowded with monasteries, in which numerous bonzes would have devoted their lives to sterile contemplation, which would have profited their country not at all. Fortunately, however, the old philosopher was succeeded by the more practical Confucius, who made China what he meant it to be during his lifetime, enforcing respect for tradition with the strict observance of the worship of ancestors. Devoted to agriculture, he did much to promote its scientific practice; an inexorable lover of justice, he had no mercy on the abuses and peculations of the mandarins. He knew how to turn to account every incident which could redound to his fame, and about his name gathered many romantic legends such as serve to fix on their hero the love and admiration of the populace. In this he differed, as did all the other great leaders of thought in the East, from Lao-Tsze, who owed his celebrity to the culte of pure reason alone, a doctrine too abstract for the apprehension of the general public, who ever delight in the marvellous. The earlier philosopher appeared and disappeared with absolutely no *éclat*, and his most ardent admirers never associated his birth or death with anything supernatural. It was far otherwise with Buddha, Confucius, Mahomet, and our Saviour, who one and all were credited with the power of working miracles, though those of Christ alone have been authenticated.

It could only detract from the real glory of Confucius to dwell on the many extraordinary phenomena which are said by his disciples to have accompanied his entrance into the world. The great Chinese dragon called *Kilin*, who never comes down to earth from his home in heaven except to foretell marvellous events, failed not to appear in the garden of the house of the future hero's father, where he vomited forth a stone of jade bearing the following inscription:

BIRTH OF CONFUCIUS

"A child as pure as the crystalline wave will be born when the dynasty of Tcheu is in its decline; he will be king, but without any kingdom."

According to the most trustworthy accounts

FIG. 24.—THE HOUSE IN WHICH CONFUCIUS WAS BORN.
(*Univers Pittoresque.*)

Confucius was born in the village of Ch'ich in the present province of Shantung in B.C. 551. The only child of his parents, he lost his father when he was but three years old, and was brought up by his mother, who was left with very little money. To quote the philosopher's own words, he could from the first "do whatever his heart prompted, and his mind was set on learning from the age of fifteen."

Before he was twenty he had attracted the

FIG. 25.—PORTRAIT OF CONFUCIUS. (*Univers Pittoresque.*)

general attention of his neighbours through the skill with which he rendered fertile districts which had long been considered barren. He was equally successful in the breeding of flocks, and the land under his care supported thousands of animals, so that the farmers who before could scarcely eke out

QUOTATION FROM CONFUCIUS

a miserable subsistence, now found themselves rich and well-to-do.

On the death of his mother he had her body transported to the grave of his father, saying: "Those who were united in life should not be separated after death." The two were therefore buried together with their heads towards the north and their feet towards the south. The remains were protected from wild beasts by being placed in strongly constructed wooden coffins, made of planks four inches thick and smeared with oil and varnish. To ensure their preservation as long as possible mounds of earth forming regular little hills were piled up above them.

During the three years of mourning which succeeded his sad loss, when, according to a custom

FIG. 26.—A FUNERAL PROCESSION IN CHINA.

still observed, he could do no public work, Confucius devoted himself to the study of ancient usage in everything connected with the death of a father or a mother.

FIG. 27.—CHINESE TOMBS.

A CHINESE TOMB.

"As man," he wrote, "is the most perfect being under heaven, that of which he is made up is worthy of the very greatest respect; as he is by nature the king of the earth, every other creature upon that earth is subject to his laws and bound to do him homage; to be indifferent to what becomes of his remains when the breath of life no longer animates those remains, is to a certain extent to degrade him from his dignity, and to reduce him to the level of the brutes. The honours you render to those you replace upon the earth will be rendered to you in your turn by those who succeed you."

During a long sojourn in the Philippine Islands, which have recently been so very much before the public in consequence of the results of the war between America and Spain, I was surprised to notice that the cemeteries were as a rule situated in the most barren and uncultivated districts. Once a year plates of rice were brought and placed upon the graves by the relatives of those interred in them. When I arrived in China, however, I found the same peculiarity the fashion there, and the last resting-places of the dead who had once resided in Canton, Macao, and other large Chinese towns were far away from the haunts of the living. The reason was explained by the sentence quoted below from the books of the great philosopher which is translated from Father Amiot's version.

It appears that some agents of Confucius had been sent by him to survey certain districts in the kingdom of Lu, and on their return they reported to him that wealthy inhabitants were in the habit of erecting sepulchres on lands which might be made very fertile.

"That is a strange abuse," cried Confucius, "and one which I mean to remedy. Burial-places should not resemble gardens of pleasure and amusement, they should be the scene of sobs and tears; it was thus that they were regarded by the ancients. To enjoy magnificent and sumptuous repasts where everything is suggestive of luxury and joy, near the tombs containing the bones of those to whom we owe our lives, is a kind of insult to the dead. These tombs must no longer be surrounded by walls, they must no longer be encircled by trees symmetrically planted. When deprived of all these frivolous ornaments, the homage which all will hasten to pay to those who have ceased to live will be sincere and pure. If, then, we desire to perform funeral rites in the spirit of their first founders we must remain true to the traditions of the sages of the remote past."

FIG. 23.—A CHINESE CEMETERY.

For the twenty-three centuries which have elapsed since this protest was written, Chinese sepulchres have always been placed on high ground of a dreary, desolate aspect, with nothing to mark them but a plain unsculptured slab of stone.

Philosophers very seldom become real friends, and the more they are thrown together the less cordial become their relations. The story goes that Confucius as a young man went to pay his respects to Lao-Tsze, but that the latter gave his visitor very haughtily to understand that he considered him wanting in humility, by which he probably meant that Confucius was too much occupied with the things of this world, and not enough with those of heaven. The fact is, that the younger reformer was interested in everything that was going on wherever he happened to be, and was ready to talk to everybody. For all that, however, he studied the most abstruse psychological problems, and I do not suppose that even Lao-Tsze himself could have made a better answer than Confucius did to the King of Lu when he asked the difficult question quoted below.

It must be remembered that in the time of Confucius, China was divided into little kingdoms, all of which the sage, who was fond of travelling, visited in turn. When he arrived at Lu, the king, who was already an old man, received him at once, and is reported to have thus addressed him:

"I have been expecting you with impatience, for I want you to explain certain things to me about nature and man. Man, our sages tell us, is distinguished from all other visible beings by the intellectual faculty which renders him capable of reasoning, and all our wise men agree in adding that man derives this valuable faculty direct from Heaven. Now is it not true that we derive our whole nature from our parents, even as other beings are reproduced by generation? I entreat you to enlighten me on this point."

"It is not easy," replied Confucius, "to explain clearly to you a matter of which so little is really known. To obey you, however, I will give you in a few words a *résumé* of all I know on the subject, and your own penetration will find out the rest.

"A portion of the substance of the father and the mother placed in the organ formed for its reception is the cause of our existence and the germ of our being. This germ would, however, remain inert and dead without the help of the two contrary principles of the Yang and the Yin.[1] These two universal agents of nature, which are in all things and everywhere, act reciprocally on it, developing it, insensibly extending and continuing it, and causing it to assume definite form.

"The germ has now become a living being, but this living being is not yet promoted to the dignity of a man; it does not become one until it is united with that intellectual substance which Heaven bestows on it to enable it to understand, to compare, and to judge. So long as this being, thus animated and endowed with intelligence, continues to combine the two principles necessary to the development, extension, the growth and the perfection of its

[1] "In the order of living beings," says M. G. Pauthier, in the section on China of *L'Univers Pittoresque*, "the Yang and the Yin are the male and female principles; in the order of the elements they are the luminous and the dark principles; in the order of natural substances the strong and the weak principles."

form, it will enjoy life; it ceases to live as soon as these two principles cease to combine. It does not attain to the fulness of life except by degrees, and by means of expansion; in the same way it is only finally destroyed by gradual decay. Its destruction is not, however, destruction properly so called, it is a decomposition into its original elements; the intellectual substance returns to the heaven whence it came; the animal breath, or the *Khi*, becomes united with the aërial fluid, whilst the earthly and liquid substances become once more earth and water.

"Man, say our ancient sages, is a unique being, in whom are united the attributes of all other beings. He is endowed with intelligence, with the power of attaining perfection, with liberty, and with social qualities; he is able to discriminate, to compare, to work for a definite aim, and to take the necessary measures for the attainment of that aim. He may become perfect or depraved according to the good or evil use he makes of his liberty; he is acquainted alike with virtue and vice, and feels that he has duties to perform towards Heaven, himself, and his fellow-men. If he acquit himself of these various duties, he is virtuous and worthy of recompense; he is culpable and merits punishment if he neglects them. This is a very short *résumé* of all I can tell you of the nature of man."

The King of Lu, it is said, was delighted with this reply, as how could he fail to be? Some years later the monarch made his sage adviser prime minister of his realm, and the philosopher remained in power for three years, administering justice so rigorously that, says one of his biographers, "if gold or jewels were dropped on the highway they would remain untouched until the rightful owner appeared to claim them." The story goes that under Confucius, Lu became so prosperous as to arouse the jealousy of the neighbouring King of Tse, who, with a wonderful insight into human nature, sent not an army, but a troop of beautiful dancing-girls to the court of the rival monarch. The manœuvre was successful; the King of Lu neglected the affairs of state to watch the posturing of the sirens, and Confucius fell into disgrace. When he proudly told his sovereign to choose between him and the dancers, the old king promptly replied that he preferred the latter, so Confucius went forth with his followers to seek his fortunes elsewhere.

Many are the anecdotes told of the wanderings of the sage after this tragic end to his work of reformation in his native state. In some districts he was gladly welcomed; in others he was often in danger of his life. At the court of Yen, where the king questioned him much as the monarch of Lu had done, he held forth less on abstruse doctrine than on education. "Young men," he is reported to have said, "should travel and become acquainted with many lands, so as to be able to judge the customs of different nations, and the peculiar characteristics of various races. I am so penetrated by this truth," he added, "that I will not fail to put it in practice whenever I get the opportunity. I would recommend the exercises of the gymnasium to all adolescents, and the study of what are called the liberal arts: Music, civil and religious ceremonial, arithmetic, fencing, and the art (*sic*) of managing skilfully a carriage of any kind drawn by horses or oxen." To his son, who asked him if he ought to devote himself to poetry, he replied: "You will never know how to speak or write well unless you make verses."

One day he met a party of hunters, and, to the great surprise of his own followers, he asked to be allowed to join them, explaining that the first inhabitants of the earth lived by the chase alone, and adding that the reason he wished to be a hunter was to impress upon those about him once more how great a respect he had for the traditions of olden times.

He learnt music when very young, and found in it a rest and recreation after his arduous and varied avocations. He became, it is said, so wonderfully skilful in the art of music, that when he had once heard the work of a composer, he could draw a faithful portrait of him, bringing out alike his physical and moral characteristics, which was indeed going to the very root of the matter. As for me, I do not think it is by any means necessary to be able to perform on an instrument in order to form a very good idea of the character of such composers as Rossini, Berlioz, and Wagner, after hearing *Il Barbiere di Siviglia*, *Les Troyens*, or *Die Meistersinger;* but as for giving portraits of their personal appearance, that would truly be difficult!

Confucius, who took to himself a wife at the age of nineteen, was in favour of early marriages, and placed the limit of age for a woman at twenty, and for a man at thirty. He founded his arguments on the fact that in China a boy is considered to have become a man directly he enters his twentieth year, and that as soon as a girl is fifteen the management of the house is entrusted to her during the winter, whilst in the spring, when ploughing begins, she is sent to look after the mulberry trees. At the respective ages of twenty and fifteen, a boy and girl may become the head of a family, "if," discreetly adds the sage, "the parents give permission."

I take a real pleasure in recalling the kindly sayings of this old-world sage, who, it must be remembered, lived 600 years before the birth of our Lord, a fact which ought to silence those who are accustomed to speak flippantly of the barbarism of past centuries. Moreover, the laws and customs advocated by Confucius had really been in force, in what was then called the "Middle State," for no less than 2500 years before the Christian era, but they had fallen into abeyance. The great philosopher was not so much an innovator as a restorer, for so lofty was the morality of the ancient laws that the Chinese people never dreamt of modifying them. Hence the extraordinary immobility of the manners and customs of the Orient, which contrasts so forcibly with the constant eagerness in the West for meaningless novelties. To give an account of the doctrines of Confucius is really to revive the traditions of the remote past, for which the Celestials have so deep a reverence. To give but one case in point: noticing that all mandarins have a phœnix with outspread wings embroidered on their robes, I inquired what it meant, and learnt to my astonishment that in the year 500 B.C. an Emperor had ordered this design to be worn by his chief officers on their breasts. The fabulous phœnix, the herald of good fortune so often seen in China, had appeared to this Emperor on his ascent to the throne; a sure symbol in the eyes of the Chinese of a prosperous reign, and the conservative Mandarins have kept up the custom of wearing a representation of the bird with outstretched wings ever since.

For the benefit of those who do not rightly reverence antiquity, I will quote a speech on the subject of marriage, addressed by Confucius to the King of Lu before the great philosopher was exiled from the kingdom he had ruled over so wisely.

"Marriage," said the sage, "is the right state for man, because it is only through marriage that he can fulfil his destiny upon earth; there is therefore nothing more honourable, nothing more worthy of his serious consideration than his power of fulfilling exactly all duties. Amongst these are some shared in common by both sexes, others which are to be performed by each sex in particular. The man is the head, it is for him to command; the woman is subject to him, it is for her to obey. It is the function of both together to imitate those operations of the heaven and the earth which combine in the production, the support, and the preservation of all things. Reciprocal tenderness, mutual confidence, truthfulness and respect, should form the foundation of their conduct; instruction and direction on the part of the husband, docility and complaisance on the part of the woman, in everything which does not interfere with the requirements of justice, propriety, and honour.

FIG. 29.—A YOUNG CHINESE MARRIED LADY.

"As society is now constituted, the woman owes all that she is to her husband. If death takes him from her, it does not make her her own mistress. As a daughter, she was under the authority of her father and mother, or failing them of the brothers older than herself; as a wife she was ruled by her husband as long as he lived; as a widow she is under the surveillance of her son, or if she has several sons, of the eldest of them, and this son, whilst ministering to her with all possible affection and respect, will shield her from all the dangers to which the weakness of her sex might expose her. Custom does not permit second marriage to a widow, but prescribes on the contrary that she should seclude herself within the precincts of her own house, and never leave it again all the rest of her life. She is forbidden to attend to any business, no matter what, outside her home. As a result she ought not to understand any such business; she will not even meddle in domestic matters unless compelled to do so by necessity, that is to say, whilst her children are still young. During the day she should avoid showing herself, by refraining from going from room to room, unless obliged to do so. And during the night the room in which she sleeps should always be lit up. Only by leading a retired life such as this will she win amongst her descendants the glory of having fulfilled the duties of a virtuous woman."

It would indeed be difficult for a widow to live up to such an ideal as this, and that the Chinese themselves realize the fact, is proved by their raising monuments to the memory of those who succeed.

"I have already said," adds Confucius, "that between fifteen and twenty is the age at which a girl should change her state by marriage. As on this change of state depends the happiness or misery in which she will pass the rest of her days, nothing should be neglected to procure for her a proper establishment, and the most advantageous one permitted by circumstances. Special care should be taken not to allow her to enter a family which has taken part in any conspiracy against the State, or in any open revolt, or into one whose affairs are in disorder, or which is agitated by internal dissensions. She should not have a husband chosen for her who has been publicly dishonoured by any crime bringing him under the notice of the law; to a man suffering from any chronic complaint, any mental eccentricity, any bodily deformity, such as would make it difficult to get on with him, or render him repulsive or disagreeable, or to a man who is the eldest of a family but has neither father nor mother. With the exception of these five classes of men, a husband may be chosen for her from any rank of society, with whom it will depend on herself alone whether she passes her life happily or not. She has but to fulfil exactly all the duties of her new state to enjoy the portion of bliss destined for her."

It is the parents who decide who their children shall marry, and a young Chinaman does not know his *fiancée* until the day of his wedding. This explains why Confucius thought it necessary to go into all these details on the subject of suitable husbands.

"A husband," he adds, "has the right to put away his wife, but he must not use this right in an arbitrary manner; he must have some legitimate cause for enforcing it. The legitimate causes of repudiation reduce themselves to seven: The first when a woman cannot live in harmony with her father- or mother-in-law; the second, if she is unable to perpetuate the race because of her recognized sterility; the third, if she be justly suspected of having violated conjugal fidelity, or if she gives any proof of unchastity; the fourth, if she bring trouble into her home by calumnious or indiscreet reports; the fifth, if she have any infirmity such as every man would naturally shrink from; the sixth, if it is difficult to correct her of the use of intemperate language; the seventh, if unknown to her husband she steals anything secretly in the house, no matter from what motive.

"Although any one of these reasons is sufficient to authorize a husband to put away his wife, there are three circumstances which forbid him to use his right: the first, when his wife has neither father nor mother, and would have nowhere to go to; the second, when she is in mourning for her father- or mother-in-law, for three years after the death of either of them; the third, when her husband, having been poor when he married her, has subsequently become rich."

Truly there is much wisdom in the counsels of Confucius on the vexed subject of marriage, but it is impossible to help feeling that the very low view he took of the position of women detracts greatly from the merit of the discourse quoted above. We are, in fact, inclined to endorse the opinion of the

FIG. 30.—A MARRIAGE PROCESSION.

missionary Gutzlaff, who, speaking of the revered sage, remarks: "By not giving a proper rank in society to females, by denying to them the privileges which are their due as sisters, mothers, wives, and daughters . . . he has marred the harmony of social life, and put a barrier against the improvement of society. The regeneration of China will, in fact, never take place, unless the females be raised from the degraded state which Confucius assigned to them."

On yet another exciting topic, that of suicide, it will perhaps be salutary to relate one anecdote illustrating the view the reformer took of the matter, now that so many despairing souls have lost the aids and consolations of religious faith in struggling with the difficulties of their life on earth; when followers of the stoical and heroic Zeno are becoming rarer and rarer, and so many young men and women resort to the fumes of charcoal, or to the waters of the nearest river, to put an end to the woes they have not the courage to face. We must premise, however, that there is really far more excuse for an Asiatic to take his own life than for a European, there being nothing unreasonable about it according to the doctrine of Buddha, whose disciples believe firmly in the transmigration of souls. They do not, it is true, profess to know whether, if they commit suicide they will become animals, but they are firmly convinced that they will continue to live, whereas the atheist has faith in nothingness alone.

In one of his many journeys Confucius and his disciples met a man who was trying to strangle himself with a rope. When asked what his motives were for wishing to commit suicide, he replied that he had been a bad son, a bad father, and a bad citizen. The remorse he felt for the terrible character his self-examination revealed him to be from all these three points of view, had made his life odious to him, and he had come out to a lonely place to put an end to it.

FIG. 31.—A DESPERATE MAN.

Greatly shocked, Confucius reproved him, addressing him in the following terms: "However great the crimes you have committed, the worst of all of them is yielding to despair. All the others may be allowed, but that is irremediable. You have, no doubt, gone astray from the very first steps you took upon earth. You should have begun by being a man of ordinary worth before attempting to distinguish yourself. You cannot attain to being an eminent person until you have strictly fulfilled the duty imposed by nature on every human creature. You ought to have begun by being a good son; to love and serve those to whom you owed your being was the most essential of your obligations; you neglected to do so, and from that negligence have resulted all your misfortunes.

"Do not, however, suppose that all is lost; take

FIG. 32.—THE TOMB OF CONFUCIUS. (*Univers Pittoresque*.)

courage again, and try to become convinced of a truth which all past centuries have proved to be incontestable. This is the truth I refer to; treasure it up in your mind, and never lose hold of it: *As long as a man has life, there is no reason to despair of him;*

he may pass suddenly from the greatest trouble to the greatest joy, from the greatest misfortune to the greatest felicity. Take courage once more, return home, and strive to turn to account every instant, as if you began to-day for the first time to realize the value of life."

Then turning to the younger of his disciples, Confucius said to them: "What you have heard from the lips of this man is an excellent lesson for you—reflect seriously upon it, every one of you."

After this remonstrance it is said that thirteen of the followers of the sage left him to return home and perform their filial duties. The Celestials, in fact, all agree in saying that filial piety was alike the groundwork of the Confucian philosophy and the foundation of Chinese society. In spite of much that is strange to European ideas, might we not well follow many of the precepts of the enlightened pre-Christian teacher?

CHAPTER V

My voyage to Macao—General appearance of the port—Gambling propensities of the Chinese—Compulsory emigration—Cruel treatment of coolies on board ship—Disaster on the Paracelses reefs—The *Baracouns*—The grotto of Camoens—The *Lusiads*—Contrast between Chinese and Japanese—Origin of the yellow races: their appearance and language—Relation of the dwellers in the Arctic regions to the people of China—Russian and Dutch intercourse with the Celestials—East India Company's monopoly of trade—Disputes on the opium question—Expiration of charter—Death of Lord Napier of a broken heart—Lin-Tseh-Hsu as Governor of the Kwang provinces—The result of his measures to suppress trade in opium—Treaty of Nanking—War of 1856-1858—Treaty of Tien-tsin and Convention of Pekin—Immense increase in exports and imports resulting from them.

I HAD confided to M. Vaucher, that most amiable of cicerones whom I had been fortunate enough to meet at Canton, my great wish to go to Macao and make a pilgrimage to the grotto where it is said Camoens, the great Portuguese poet, wrote a portion of his most important work, the *Lusiads*. M. Vaucher at once made arrangements for me to go to the celebrated Portuguese settlement by river and sea, and placed one of his own decked boats at my disposal. He even went so far as to choose a crew for me, and to arm that crew with six rifles. Before I started he warned me to keep in my cabin so as not to arouse the cupidity of the banditti, who abound on the river, by appearing on deck.

"If," he said to me, "my men point out to you a suspicious-looking craft, be on your guard against it. You may easily," he added, "recognize pirate boats for yourself, for this reason, they always prowl about in groups of three, so that each may help the others in case of bad weather or any difficulty; a clever arrangement greatly facilitating their evil designs, for the crews are rapidly transformed from harmless fishermen to fierce pirates should occasion serve for doing a stroke of business."

In spite of these ominous warnings, however, my voyage passed over without incident, and I arrived safely at the port of Macao, situated on the southern extremity of a small peninsula of the island of Hiang-shang and separated from the Chinese province of Canton merely by a wall, which is in as ruinous a condition as is the more celebrated Great Wall of Tartary. As we approached Macao a beautiful scene was spread out before us, wooded hills dotted with charming villas, in which the wealthy English of Hong-Kong spend much of the summer, and groups of picturesque rocks rising from the curving shores of the lovely bay with its

EMIGRATION AGENTS

stretch of gleaming white sand, to which the Portuguese, to whom Macao was ceded by the Chinese, have given the appropriate name of the *Porto de Praya grande.*

Here swarms the teeming amphibious fishing population of Macao, and from this perfect bow with its picturesque surroundings were shipped, alas! for all too many years, thousands of coolies for the labour market of Havana and Peru, who were many of them embarked under terribly tragic circumstances.

A true Celestial is in fact a born gambler, and indulges his instincts to such an extent that when he has lost fortune, wife, and daughters he finally stakes himself! This fact is well known to the emigration agents not only of Macao, but of the other Chinese ports, where numbers were formerly enrolled for service in Peru, Chili, the Philippine Islands, and various places in Oceania with very little, if any, volition on their own part. Emigration agents used to lie in wait for Chinese loungers, and accost those who looked fairly robust politely, take them to the flower-boats and other public resorts where opium was smoked, and if their luckless victims still had any money left, their insinuating tempters would entice them into some low gambling hell, where, after a few throws of the dice, the ruin of the simple, confiding fellows was complete. Then when the unfortunate Celestials had emptied their purses, and their brains were muddled with opium or from the effects of debauchery, their dim eyes were dazzled by the offer of a few piastres, and in exchange for a trifling sum they signed away their liberty. When they came to their senses they found they had bound themselves to leave their country.

The agents were careful when they got the poor fellows' signatures not to let out how far from China were the sugar-cane plantations of the Antilles or the guano isles of Peru. Their victims had only learnt one fact thoroughly, and that was that their country is the centre of the universe, the foreign nations surrounding it being looked upon as its tributaries. If the emigrants asked where they were going, they were told to some place very near the port of embarkation. This wicked deception was really the cause of the terrible massacres of coolies to which many captains of emigrant vessels were driven to save their ships and crews. When after a few days' voyage a vessel had to touch at some port for any reason, and the poor coolies packed away below the hatchways saw above the barriers or through the portholes, the bright verdure of an island of Oceania, or the distant blue mountains of the American continent, they at once jumped to the conclusion that their journey was at an end, and were wild to leave the vessel, no matter at what cost. Some even in mid-ocean, out of sight of land, became so heartbroken from home-sickness that they quietly packed up the few things belonging to them and jumped into the sea with them. Now and then a few of these would-be suicides were fished out again by order of the captain, and would calmly explain their action by some such speech as this: "We want to go back to our own country." Truly those who believe in metempsychosis cherish wonderful delusions!

On one occasion in the roadstead of Manila a swarm of coolies who thought they had arrived at Havana mutinied because the captain would not allow them to land. The crew of the vessel drove them back between decks at the point of the sword, and they all perished from suffocation in a few hours for want of air.

Mutiny on their part was not, however, the only reason which sometimes led to the sacrifice of a whole cargo of Asiatics. It was all too often a case of might makes right, and when some convulsion of the elements rendered it imperative to lighten a vessel, many a captain easily persuaded himself that he had no choice but to save his crew by the sacrifice of his human freight. This was the cause of the awful catastrophe off the Paracelses reefs in the China Sea, which have as sinister a reputation as the Goodwin Sands of the English coast, or the Baie des Trépassés of that of Brittany. An unskilful captain had run his vessel on to the far-famed reefs during the night, and seeing that it was hopeless to attempt to save the five hundred coolies he was to have taken to Peru, he called his crew together and told them to lower all the boats as quietly as possible. This was done, and the captain saved himself and his sailors, leaving the five hundred Celestials to their fate. The unfortunate coolies, roused from their sleep by the bumping of the vessel against the rocks, uttered piercing screams for help from the narrow space in which they were confined, but we need scarcely add that the cautious captain had most likely had the hatchways securely nailed down by his carpenter before he left the ship.

When there is not much sea on, the Paracelses reefs can be clearly seen, certain flat portions emerging here and there for a few inches above the surface of the water. If there were never such a thing as a storm, and no danger of the islets being swept by the waves, it would be possible to live on them and even to support life by feeding on the turtles and shell-fish abounding there; so that if the poor abandoned coolies had been able to get out of their prison, who can tell but what they might have saved themselves by clinging to the rocks till help arrived? As it was, however, not a single emigrant was ever seen again. On the arrival safe and sound at Hong-Kong of the captain and his crew, the English authorities at once sent the fleetest steamer in the port to the scene of the shipwreck, but those on that steamer saw nothing of the lost vessel, which must have been quickly dashed to pieces. The Paracelses reefs were completely under water, masses of surging foam hiding all trace of them, so that had any of the coolies landed it would only have been to be swept quickly away to the open sea by the force of the current.

Perhaps the saddest part of the tragedy was that the fate of so many human creatures who had disappeared for ever in the depths of that blind and reckless destroyer, the Ocean, should have raised so little regret, either amongst the white-skinned traders in human flesh or the yellow-faced Celestials of Macao and Hong-Kong. Maybe the latter themselves realize that they really are too prolific, and are not sorry when their numbers are lessened, no matter by what means.

When I was at Macao, I saw some of the so-called *baracouns*, where the emigrants used to be shut up whilst awaiting their embarcation. These *baracouns* are the disused vaults of old convents, damp cellars of vast extent, which were closed with strong bars when in use as pens for human cattle. I am thankful to say these barracks are empty now, and are no longer hot-beds of disease, for the European powers have interfered to put a stop to the infamous traffic. It is a great gratification to me to know, on the authority of the Quai d'Orsay officials, that an indignant article on the subject, which I contributed to the *Revue des Deux Mondes*, had something to do with this most desirable step.

Emigration still goes on, on a very large scale, but it is conducted in a less barbarous manner. No Chinese can now be made to embark against his will, and his signature to a contract no longer compels him to leave his native land if he has any means of support. As time goes on, it is to be hoped that something like true liberty will really be the heritage of the Chinese people, and already, where European ideas are gaining ground, there are glimmerings of the dawn of a better state of things.

In China, as elsewhere, the glory of the Portuguese colonies is departed, and the settlement at Macao is no exception to the rule. For many years the name of that port was synonymous with decay and degradation. The native population was more debased; the foreign traders were more grasping, more greedy of gain, and more reckless of the means employed to secure it than anywhere else, and one tricolour flag, floating above a hospital for invalid sailors, was the only note of true civilization to redeem a deplorable state of things. The Sisters of Charity, who had come all the way from France to soothe the sufferings of European mariners in a strange land, taught the people of Macao that there was another love than that of the piastre, another intoxication than that produced by the fumes of opium: the love of helping others, the intoxication of zeal for humanity. The much-abused and hated Macao is now the seat of a bishop and the head-quarters of French missionary effort in China, whilst the export trade has passed from the hands of the Portuguese into that of the British, a truly beneficent change for all concerned.

My visit to the horrible *baracouns* made me quite miserable, so vividly did they bring before me all the horrors of the but recently-changed system of compulsory emigration. I did my best to forget

them; and on the eve of my departure from Macao
I went to see the grotto associated with the name
of Camoens. It will be remembered that the poet
was banished to Macao in 1556 on account of his
quarrel with the authorities at Goa, whither he had
been sent after the fracas in the streets of Lisbon,
in which he wounded a royal equerry. He seems
on the whole to have enjoyed his exile, for he
obtained a post with a large salary, and in two
years made quite a fortune. This so-called grotto
is not really a cave now, whatever it may originally
have been, but is a picturesque little building
perched on a site commanding a beautiful view of the
bay and its shipping. Truly a fitting scene to inspire
the rhapsody in which Camoens celebrated the glory
of his fellow-countryman, Vasco da Gama, and be-
moaned the sad fate of the beautiful Iñez de
Castro, who, the story goes, after being for some ten
years the mistress of the Infante of Portugal, Dom
Pedro, was secretly married to him in 1354, and
murdered by order of her father-in-law in 1355.
When the bereaved husband came to the throne
he put two of the murderers of his bride to death
by torture; and, according to Camoens, had the
dead body of Iñez exhumed, dressed in royal robes,
and placed upon the throne she would have
occupied had she lived, to receive homage from
the court.

In the *Lusiads*, which has been called the "Epos
of Commerce," and is to the Portuguese what
Chaucer's *Canterbury Tales* is to the English, a

vivid picture is given of the grandeur of the poet's native country in the fifteenth century, when it was the rival of Spain, and a leader in the colonization of distant lands. Perhaps one of the finest passages of this remarkable poem, or series of poems, is that in which its author invokes the mighty spirit of the storm, Adamastor, the fierce guardian of the Cape of Good Hope, over whom Vasco da Gama and Magellan, also of Portuguese birth, both triumphed. Now that time has proved how fatal to the real welfare of both Spain and Portugal was the wealth of India and of Mexico, one cannot help feeling that the poet may perhaps have had something of a prophetic intuition of the future decadence of the peninsular kingdoms, when he placed a giant in the pathway of the Conquistadores, to bar the way against them.

It has only been for the last forty years that either China or Japan can be said to have been open to Europeans. The history of the latter nation is a proof of what an active, brave, and intelligent people may achieve in the course of a few years; whilst that of the former illustrates all that may remain undone where the natives of a country are convinced that they have for forty centuries had an ideal government, the best possible religion, and that the products of their industries are quite incapable of improvement.

In passing judgment on the Chinese it must, however, be borne in mind that their country is, by its natural boundaries, so completely isolated from the rest of the world as to justify to some extent their intense reluctance to open relations with the Red Devils of the West, as they call all Europeans, whether fair or dark, though it was evidently the bright auburn hair and rosy complexions of so many of the English visitors to China which originated the name. The giving of this title is the only vengeance the poor yellow skins have been able to take on those who invaded their capital, pillaged their palaces and burnt their arsenals and vessels, not to speak of the importation of the pernicious drug, opium, which is responsible for the death of thousands every year.

Independently of the Great Wall which once, though not very successfully, defended China from the incursions of the Mongols and Manchus, the Celestial Empire is bounded on the north by the great Gobi desert and the grass steppes of Southern Mongolia; on the east by the sea of China, the Eastern and the Yellow Seas; whilst on the west rise many a lofty chain of mountains, their summits almost always crowned with snow. These latter have not yet been all fully explored, though the name of many a hero of discovery is connected with them, including that of Prince Henry of Orleans, Margary and Marcel Monnier of quite recent fame.

In the vast circle enclosed within these boundaries of desert, mountain, and sea, nearly every kind of vegetation can be successfully cultivated in one district or another, whilst a considerable variety of types of the great human family is met with, including members belonging to the same groups as the people who have poured into Corea, Japan, Formosa, the Philippine Islands, Indo-China, Siam, Kulja, and even a country so far away as Persia.

As is well known, anthropologists are divided into two absolutely distinct camps: the Polygenists, who claim that differences of species evidenced by differences in height, in features, and in complexion, are the result of the springing of the human race from different progenitors; and the Monogenists, who believe in one primæval pair of parents only, and look upon all differences between human creatures as caused by accidental conditions modifying the primitive type. The latter assert that it was within the boundaries mentioned above, on the central plateau of the present Celestial Empire, that the first men appeared, and as they multiplied, became diversified into yellow, black, white, and red, remaining in their primitive home until, like a cup filled too full, they overflowed in every direction to people other lands.

It is not for me to decide the vexed question of whether the polygenists or monogenists are in the right; those curious on the subject may refer to the learned and deeply interesting works of Quatrefages, Haeckel, Darwin, Huxley, Wallace and others, who have brought their critical acumen to bear on the subject of the origin and antiquity of man. I merely wish to emphasize here the fact that all agree in believing China to have been

THE MONGOLIANS

occupied at an extremely remote date, and in admitting that, however the changes may have come about, the human family is now undoubtedly divided into five distinct groups: the brown, the black, the red, the white, and the yellow. To the last belong the Mongolians, with whom alone we have now to do, and which numbers, whatever its peculiarities, more representatives than any other at the present day.

The skin of this prolific race is always yellow, sometimes pale, and sometimes of a brownish tinge. The stiff straight hair of the Mongol is as black as ebony, and the skull is of the so-called bracycephalic type, that is to say, short as compared to its breadth, whilst that of the Chinese and Tartars is mesaticephalic, or of medium length and breadth.

The face is round, the eyes are mere narrow slits, often decidedly oblique, the nose is large, the cheek-bones are very prominent, and the lips are thick.

At first sight it would appear that the Mongolian dialects all spring from one primitive speech, but examination of evidence proves that this is not the case, for they really belong to two very ancient branches of human speech: the monosyllabic language of the Indo-Chinese races, and the polysyllabic of the other Mongolians. The Tibetans, Burmans, Siamese, and Chinese dialects are all monosyllabic, whilst those in use by the Coreans, Japanese, Tartars, Kirghizes, Kalmucks, Buriats, Samoyedes, and Finns are polysyllabic.

All the inhabitants of the continent of Asia, with the exception of a few tribes of the extreme north, certain groups of Malays and Dravidians in India, with some of the dwellers in the Mediterranean districts of the south-west, belong to the so-called *Homo mongolicus*, or Mongolian branch of the great human family, whilst in Europe it claims the Finns and Lapps of the north, the Osmanlis of Turkey, and the Magyars of Hungary. *Homo articus*, or the Polar group, is considered by the best authorities to have originally formed part of the Mongolian branch, including the Esquimaux, the Greenlanders, the Kamtchatkans, etc., all of whom, however, as pointed out by Haeckel, the great German naturalist, have in the course of centuries become so modified by the conditions of life in the Arctic regions, that they may now be looked upon as forming a separate species.

The inhabitants of the extreme north are short and squat, their skulls are of the mesaticephalic, or even in some cases of the dolichocephalic type, that is to say, they are long in proportion to their breadth; their eyes are narrow and oblique, as are those of the Mongols; they have high cheek-bones and large mouths. Their hair is coarse and black, and their skin of a more or less clear brown colour, sometimes approaching to white, and sometimes to yellow, as amongst the Mongols, whilst now and then it is reddish, as is that of the native Americans. The dialects spoken by these remote tribes differ as much from those of other Mongols as they do from the American forms of speech, and the probability is that these inhabitants of the Arctic regions are really a degenerate branch of the Mongol race, whose progenitors passed over into the north of America from the north-east of Asia.

In spite of the fact that emigrants did occasionally drift across the formidable northern and western boundaries of the vast Celestial Empire, the one leading idea for many centuries, alike of rulers and ruled, was to keep their land sacred from intruders, and discourage all intercourse with other nations, whom the Chinese were trained from infancy to look upon as utter barbarians. There is no more thrilling or more interesting story in literature than that of how this cherished isolation was in the end broken in upon and the delusion finally dispelled, that Europe was but a small, sparsely populated district, whose inhabitants were eager to trade with the yellow men because of the poverty of their own land.

The Russians and the Dutch, as well as the Portuguese, were eager in the seventeenth and eighteenth centuries to trade with China, and plant permanent colonies within its boundaries, but self-interest alone prompted their efforts, and they did nothing to open the eyes of the natives to the true character of western civilization. The French, however, to their honour be it spoken, were the pioneers of missionary effort, and as has been well pointed out by Archibald Colquhoun in his *China in*

Transformation, page 43, "the earlier knowledge of the West acquired by China, and that of China acquired by the West, were mainly achieved by French missionaries ; no French Government ever sent a mission to Pekin to seek merely advantages of trade," and it was not until 1869 that a different policy was inaugurated. Far different was it with the English who obtained a footing in China, for from the very first their one aim was to trade upon the ignorance of the natives, and to make the largest possible fortunes. British trade with China began later than that of the other great Western powers, but it rapidly grew to far greater importance than that of Russia or Portugal, chiefly because it was mainly carried on by that great and powerful commercial body, the East India Company, on whom rests the responsibility of the first introduction to the Celestial Empire of opium, now consumed in such immense quantities and cultivated in China itself, but which was totally unknown there before the eighteenth century. For over two centuries the East India Company enjoyed a monopoly of trade, and in their eagerness for gain its members swallowed many an affront to their own and their country's dignity, for their relations to the Chinese Government resembled those of humble suppliants to the "Son of Heaven."

There is something deeply pathetic in the gradual realization by that "Son of Heaven" that the sons of earth from over the sea were really more powerful than himself, and that he was the one to be defeated in any real conflict with them. How touching, for instance, was the edict issued in 1800, the first year of the century, so fatal to China as a nation, prohibiting the importation of opium, an edict utterly powerless to check the evil, which was spreading like a fatal blight throughout the length and breadth of the doomed land. The traffic went on unchecked, and between 1821 and 1831 the amount landed at the various ports increased from 4628 chests to 23,670. In 1832 the monopoly of the Company came to an end, and the heads of the factories were succeeded by a representative of the Sovereign of Great Britain, whom the Chinese authorities hoped to coerce more easily than they could the many-headed hydra the Company had seemed to be. "On the one side," says Professor Legge, "was a resistless force determined to prosecute its enterprise for the enlargement of its trade, and the conduct of it as with an equal nation; on the other side, was the old Empire seeming to be unconscious of its weakness, determined not to acknowledge the claim of equality, and confident of its power to suppress the import of opium." For a brief space it seemed as if the latter would gain the day, for England made the fatal mistake of associating with her first representative, Lord Napier, two men who had been in the hated East India Company. The policy pursued was weak and vacillating; Lord Napier was disowned by his Government, and after suffering much indignity at the hands of the Chinese, died at Macao of a broken heart. He was succeeded by Sir J. F. Davis, during whose term of office the relations between the two countries became more and more strained, until in 1839 the Chinese Government made its last final effort to oust out alike the foreigners and the abuses they had introduced, which were to it as an ever-present canker eating into the life of the nation. The able politician, Lin-Tseh-Hsu, was appointed Governor-General of the Kwang provinces with orders to bring the foreign devils to reason.

It so happened when the new ruler, who was "a thoroughly orthodox Chinaman," arrived at Canton, there were British ships in port with some twenty thousand chests of opium on board. Lin at once ordered these to be given up for destruction, and as no notice was taken of his demand, he commanded all the Chinese in the service of the foreigners to leave them at once. They dared not disobey, and when they were gone a cordon of troops was posted round the British quarters, and a manifesto was issued to the effect that unless the opium was surrendered all the merchants would be slain. Captain Eliot, who was Secretary to Sir J. F. Davis, seeing no hope of rescue, gave up the opium, which was flung with quantities of quick-lime, salt and water into deep trenches at Chunhow, near the mouth of the river, "where it quickly became decomposed, and the mixture ran into the sea."

This and other high-handed measures of the energetic Governor of Kwang led to the war which resulted in the ceding of Hong-Kong to the English and the opening to British trade of Canton, Amoy, Fuchan, Ningpo, and Shanghai. The spell was in fact finally broken, Chinese isolation was at an end for ever, and the first chapter was written of the history of modern China. China is a land doomed to partition amongst the hated "foreign devils," who are eager to divide the spoil, and are preparing to intersect the once sacred interior of the flowery land with the relentless iron roads, before the advance of which all privacy and seclusion disappear.

The Treaty of Nanking, signed in 1842, was succeeded after another war, which began in 1856 and ended in 1858, by the Treaty of Tien-tsin, making yet further concessions to England; but it was not until after the Anglo-French Expedition had crossed the Pei-Ho river, and encamped beneath the very walls of the capital itself, that the Chinese realized how futile was further resistance. The Convention of Pekin, signed in 1860, ratified the Treaty of Tien-tsin, and formed the foundation of the present relations between China and Great Britain. The Emperor, Hsien-Fung, died the next year, and his last hours must indeed have been embittered by the knowledge that the flood-gates were opened, and that he could only leave the semblance of power to his successor, an infant of five years old. Nothing could now check the introduction of European civilization, which in the eyes of the Chinese was synonymous with all that was most detrimental to their true interests.

Fortunately, however, the advantages were not really so entirely on the side of the foreigners as is generally supposed; for the people will in the end, it is hoped, lead better and nobler lives than before. Missionaries of many nationalities are doing their best against terrible odds to introduce the religion of the Redeemer, and even in material matters some good has resulted to the much-oppressed natives. Numerous steamers have long plied unmolested to and fro between the chief European ports and Shanghai, and a system of custom-house control has been established in that important town of Central China, greatly to the advantage of native trade. The taxes imposed on foreign goods are now one of the most important sources of the revenues of the Empire, and the driving away of the "foreign devils" would mean an incalculable loss to the Chinese themselves. The total value of the exports from Shanghai alone is more than £22,715,000, of which some £8,746,000 represents native produce from the immediate neighbourhood of the port, whilst the imports, including Chinese goods from other districts, reaches a considerably higher figure. All this means prosperity to the millions, who before the throwing open of the inland provinces to foreign commerce, lived from hand to mouth, and were ground down by the ceaseless exactions of the native officials. This truth is not unfortunately even now really understood by the populace, for political knowledge filters very slowly from the palace to the hovels of China; but we may yet hope to see the day when really cordial relations will be established between the white and yellow races. The defeat of China by Japan, with the huge indemnity exacted by the latter, was of course a terrible blow to commerce; but already there are signs of recovery, for the wealth and numbers of the people of the vast Empire are really alike inexhaustible.

CHAPTER VI

French aspirations in Tonkin—Margary receives his instructions—Work already done on the Yang-tse—Margary is insulted at Paï-Chou—He awaits instructions in vain at Lo-Shan—The Tung-Ting lake—A Chinese caravanserai—The explorer leaves the river to proceed by land—He meets a starving missionary—Kwei-Chou and the French bishop there—A terrible road—Arrival at the capital of Yunnan—Armed escort from Bhâmo—Meeting between Margary and Colonel Browne—Threatening attitude of natives — Margary crosses the frontier alone — Colonel Browne's camp surrounded — Murder of Margary outside Manwyne—Importance of Yunnan and Szechuan to Europeans.

WHETHER, as has been asserted by more than one French writer, it was the French operations in Tonkin which so roused the jealousy of the British as to determine them at all risks to render those operations futile in the opening of a direct route from Yunnan to Burma, or whether they were merely pursuing their usual astute policy of making exploration precede the flag, there is no doubt that the tragic fate of the young explorer, Margary, whose adventurous journey deserves relation here, was fruitful in most important political results alike to England and to France. The French, who looked upon Tonkin as their own special key to China, had meant to make the Song-coi, or Red River, which is its chief artery, the outlet of the wealth of Yunnan; the English succeeded in making the Yang-tse that outlet by the concessions they wrung from the Chinese as part of the indemnity for the murder of their explorer.

It was in 1874 that Augustus Raimond Margary, an *attaché* of the British Embassy at Pekin, received instructions from Sir Thomas Wade, then Minister Plenipotentiary to China, to go to Bhâmo, and there meet Colonel Browne, who was about to start on an expedition across Western China, with a view to open the overland route between Burma and the Celestial Empire. Margary, who knew the natives well, and had on many occasions given proof of his tact in dealing with them, was to act as interpreter and guide to the English party.

Already the Yang-tse, the great river at the mouth of which Shanghai is situated, had been opened to foreign trade as far as Hankow, that is to say, for 600 miles, but the difficulties of communication with the interior were still immense, so bad were the roads, and so ignorant the people of the districts those roads traversed. What was really needed in the interests of British trade was a continuous route partly by water and partly by land from the port to Burma, and Margary was to test the practicability of such a route, although the brutality of the natives to foreigners was well known, and much of the district he had to traverse had never before been visited by a European. Even now, as those who have read Marcel Monnier's account of his adventures in Yunnan in the pages of the French journal *Le Temps* know full well, there is anything but a cordial feeling for foreigners in Yunnan, and a quarter of a century ago the traveller who ventured far from Hankow must have carried his life in his hand.

Nothing daunted, however, by all he knew of the perils before him, the gallant young explorer left Shanghai in a little American steamer on August 24th, accompanied only by one English servant and a Chinese secretary. Arrived at Hankow, which, now that it is to be connected with Pekin, Russian Siberia and Tonkin by rail, has a great future before it as a commercial centre, the little party left the steamer and hired boats from a native banker for the further voyage. They started again on September 4th, and on the 6th cast anchor off Païf-Chou, a picturesque town rising from amongst magnificent trees. This town turned out to be extremely well built, and prosperous, and to be surrounded by well-cultivated plantations, yielding quantities of valuable produce. Margary and his secretary wandered about for some time, noting everything, and at first the natives were very civil; but when the visitors approached the quay, to which the junks of the inhabitants were

MARGARY IN DANGER

moored, the crowd became insulting, and followed the travellers to their vessel, hooting them and dancing round them with menacing gestures. They escaped without injury, however, and pushed on to Lu-Chi-Ku, where they saw a big war-junk, with no less than twenty-one guns. On September 11th they reached Lo-Shan, where a halt was made to await a reply to a telegram sent by Margary to Sir Thomas Wade. No answer came, however, and a whole week was wasted, during which Margary nearly lost his life in a fracas with the natives. The heat was intense, and but for the shade of the fine mulberry trees on the banks of the river, would have been almost insupportable. In spite of it the Englishman spent most of his time shooting the plentiful game, consisting chiefly of partridges and pheasants. One day he had left his gun behind him, to go and call on a mandarin, who held an official post at Lo-Shan. As he was being carried in a sedan-chair by native porters, he suddenly met a gang of conscripts bound for Formosa, who surrounded him, shouting, "Ha! Ha! here is a foreign devil—let us do for the foreign devil!" How the "foreign devil" wished he had had his stout club in his hand, he would quickly have dispersed the cowardly mob; but seeing he was absolutely defenceless, the soldiers seized the ends of the bamboo rods supporting the chair, and began shaking its occupant about in a most unpleasant manner. With a quiet smile on his lips, but hatred in his heart, Margary was meditating a blow with his clenched fist in the face of the ringleader, when his servant relieved the tension of the situation by striking one of the assailants in the chest with all his force. The result was magical and immediate, the brave soldiers all ran away, and the "foreign devil" arrived safely at the house of the mandarin. Fortunately that official proved friendly, and gave his visitor the escort of two lictors for his return on board. Back again in his own boat, the

FIG. 33.—CHINESE PEASANT CRUSHING RICE.

explorer harangued the crowd, which still lingered on the bank, in these words: "Why did you treat me so roughly? Is this your politeness to strangers? I had heard that the Chinese were distinguished amongst other nations for their courtesy. Is this how you show it? Shall I go and tell my fellow-countrymen how you treat me?" This speech, in their own language, greatly astonished the audience, who received it in silence, and quietly withdrew, apparently quite ashamed of themselves, the older amongst them trying to lay the blame on the younger.

On September 20th Margary gave up all hope of hearing from Sir Thomas Wade, and resumed his voyage, feeling rather out of heart, no doubt, at the silence of his chief. Helped by a strong wind from the north-east, he succeeded the same day in leaving the muddy Yang-tse, and entering the beautiful Tung-Ting lake, of a lovely blue colour, from which the Great River draws its chief volume. At the entrance to this lovely sheet of water is the island of Chün-Shan, celebrated throughout the Celestial Empire for its tea, considered the best in China, a portion of which is set apart for the use of the Son of Heaven, or the Emperor, and for the chief dignitaries of the province in which it is grown. The lake, lovely as it is in appearance, is of little depth, and except for the clouds of venomous insects which hover over it, inflicting torture on those who venture to navigate it, there is but little life about it. A few towns of no particular importance rise from its banks, but Margary did not land at any of them. The natives of the shores of the lake say that the flies which haunt the surface of the water are the winged guardians, appointed by the Spirit of the Lake, to keep away intruders.

On the 22nd the explorer entered the river Yuen, a stream of transparent waters, and halted for a brief time opposite the town of Nih-sin-Tang, where, to his relief, the winged and barbed sentinels of the lake melted away as rapidly as they had appeared.

The banks of the Yuen are extremely picturesque: instead of the sewers and rugged paths which generally disfigure the banks of the water-courses of China, the riverine districts consist of well-cultivated land, cotton plantations alternating with beautiful meadows bordered by venerable willows. The farms, too, are clean and well kept; men, women and children seem to lead happy, prosperous lives, and Margary was everywhere kindly received. At sunrise, on the 28th, the expedition arrived opposite Tao-Yuen-Hsien, a large, prosperous, but unwalled town. This was the first important place without fortifications which Margary had visited. The inhabitants seemed very independent, and their chief industry was the making of pottery; every house, of whatever size, was decorated inside and out with tasty vases, serving as pots for the dwarf

FIG. 34.—A CHINESE FERRYMAN.

orange trees and other stunted plants in which the Chinese take so great a delight.

Beyond Tao-Yuen-Hsien the river narrows, and flows between rocky gorges, beyond which low conical hills, covered with sombre pines, rise one above the other, none of them more than about 200 feet high, the effect of which is, nevertheless, extremely fine. From the description given of the scenery by Margary, it must greatly resemble that of Civet in the Ardennes, immortalized by George Sand in her poetical romance, *Malgré tout*.

The province of Hunan, so rich in geological interest, and in which such terrible convulsions must have taken place in the remote past, was now entered, and the important town of Yuping-Hsien was soon reached, where the drooping spirits of Margary were cheered by finding the chief magistrate to be an old friend of his, who had formerly been interpreter in the English legation at Pekin. The native official received his former colleague with a salute from three guns, and, better still, wished him to spend a few days with him at his own residence. Margary gladly accepted the hospitality offered, donned his dress-uniform, and was carried in state to the Yamin or house of the magistrate, where a great crowd was assembled to witness the arrival of the foreigner.

Refreshed by his rest, the English explorer soon started again, and on October 27th reached the important town of Chen-Yuan-Fu, at the entrance to which is a very fine bridge of six arches, which would be considered a work of art even in Europe. Round about the city rise rocky heights, which give it a very picturesque appearance. Margary landed near the bridge, for he would now have to travel by land, and accompanied by his own servant and four men who had been told off to protect him, he made his way to a house where he hoped to be able to spend the night. It was not exactly a hotel, but a stopping-place where travellers could hire sedan-chairs, coolies, and horses; in fact, all that was needed for the further prosecution of his journey. As there are generally several such establishments in every important place, the Chinese proprietors always send agents down to the landing-stages to secure the custom of travellers just as do their brethren in Europe. Now the messenger who had got Margary to promise to patronize his master's house, had disappeared as soon as he had transacted the business in hand, leaving the English traveller and his men in the lurch. It was only with the greatest difficulty that the little party made their way to the caravanserai chosen, through the crowds assembled to stare at them. Arrived there, they found a clean, comfortable-looking shelter, but no one to receive them. The next thing to do was to get the baggage of the expedition under shelter, but to this the crowd outside objected so very vigorously that Margary was obliged to give up the attempt. He determined, however, to seek the aid and protection of the Hsien, or first magistrate of the town, and to

A RAGING MULTITUDE

force his way to him in spite of all opposition. He had the door of the caravanserai opened, and faced the raging multitude outside with head erect and an air of such determined resolution, that the easily daunted Chinese recoiled before him, and withdrawing as he advanced, allowed him to reach the

FIG. 35.—A MANDARIN'S HOUSE.

Yamin unhurt. There he found the chief magistrate, who must have heard all the noise, for the caravanserai was only some two hundred paces off, quietly awaiting events without moving a finger to control them.

Margary could not persuade the official to let him remain for a night's rest in the town, but he did succeed in securing four sturdy coolies as porters, by whom he was carried from Chen-Yuan, where he had been so grossly insulted, to Kwei-Yang, capital of the province of Kwei-Chou, receiving a kind welcome everywhere *en route.*

Three days before his arrival at Yunnan, capital of the province of the same name, as the English explorer was taking his lunch *al fresco,* he was, to his great surprise and delight, accosted by a Frenchman, an unfortunate missionary, who was bound for the same place, and was nearly wild with joy at finding another European in this remote district. An eager conversation began in Chinese, but as Margary could speak French, the native language was soon exchanged for it. Margary tells how the two sat down to the same " table," and were to share their meal, but the missionary was so badly off for provisions that, in the end, the Englishman gave him half his beefsteak, with all the bread he had. Then he had an omelette made for his guest, and gave him a glass of spirits. From the eagerness with which the food was consumed it was evident that the poor fellow had been almost starving. The meal over, Margary told his new friend of the way in which he had been insulted at Chen-Yuan, and the Frenchman replied that most likely the magistrate had taken the explorer for a Jesuit father, or a Lazarist, that is to say, a follower of Saint Vincent de Paul. However it may be in the future, the people of Central China had in Margary's time no toleration for Roman

Catholic missionaries, and there was little chance of their doing anything to promote civilization amongst the natives. Had the magistrate looked at the Englishman's passport when the latter first landed he would have been very differently treated. It will be traders, not preachers of the gospel, who will be the first to introduce European ideas. Even manufacturers and engineers who elsewhere often achieve so much success have little chance in China, for the people are as content with their own systems of mechanical production and their clumsy primitive modes of working their salt and mineral mines as they are with their religion.

At Hwei-Chow, a picturesque walled city of great importance, Margary met an old French bishop and two of his priests who had adopted the costume of the Chinese, and spoke their language even better than their own. The bishop, in fact, had been so long expatriated that he had forgotten his own tongue, and spoke that of his adopted country with his visitor. In fact, instead of converting the natives he had become almost a native himself, a sad fate for a once ardent missionary. He lived in a Yamin and used a green arm-chair, a privilege accorded generally to officials of Chinese birth only. He was even called Ta-jin, or a great man, a title reserved, as a rule, for mandarins of the first class. Though this assumption of native titles cannot but have been displeasing to the literati and officials, the fact that the bishop was left unmolested is a singular instance of tolerance; for what would

K

be thought in Europe of a Chinaman who should venture to adopt the uniform of a general or the robes of a cardinal? Would not steps be taken at once to despoil him of his borrowed plumes?

It was now three months since Margary had left Shanghai, and forty-nine days more would be required before he could reach Bhâmo on the Irrawadi, where he hoped to meet Colonel Browne, with whom he was to make the return journey, if the Chinese authorities would give the necessary permission. There seemed no reason to suppose that it would be refused, for nothing could have been more cordial than the reception of the young Englishman in the capital of Yunnan.

The road from Yunnan-Fow to Tali-Fow was really little more than a goat-track, and Margary gives an amusing account of his own sufferings and those of two mandarins who made the journey with him, as he was jolted along amongst the crowds of carts, mules, and donkeys which blocked the way, all alike laden with bags of salt. The Englishmen and the literati had many a laugh together over their misfortunes, and the way he made friends with pretty well every one he met speaks volumes for the tact of the explorer, who deserved a better fate than that which eventually befell him.

It was now December, and the cold was intense, but it was impossible to procure winter clothing, and the travellers had to make the best of what they happened to have with them. As Chen-nan was four days' journey from Tali-Fow, the mandarins did all they could to dissuade Margary from going further, assuring him that the people of the last-named town were very hostile to foreigners; but the Englishman, anxious to ascertain the truth about native feeling for Europeans from actual observation, was not to be deterred. On the 16th December he boldly entered the city of inhospitable reputation, and wrote in his journal: *Veni, vidi, vici!* He was unmolested, and weary though he was, he remained but one night to rest, pushing on the next day for the Burmese frontier. He reached Manwyne, the scene soon afterwards of his assassination, on January 11th, and there found an escort of forty soldiers from Burma sent to him by Colonel Browne to protect him from attack by the tribes of the frontier districts through which he had now to pass. It is very probable that the sudden appearance of all these armed men was really the cause of Margary's death. Alone, the gallant young explorer would have conciliated the friendship of the natives as he had so often done before, but surrounded by his guard he naturally became an object of suspicion.

Margary did, however, succeed in reaching Bhâmo, and suspecting no danger, he and Colonel Browne started on the return journey early in February, reaching on the 18th of that month the last post in Burma, just beyond the Chinese frontier. There the travellers learnt that the pass into Yunnan was blocked by an armed band of Kakhyens, whose opposition to the re-entry into China of the white men, if not exactly instigated was certainly connived at by the authorities of the frontier town of Seray, and also by those of Manwyne. Colonel Browne and Margary consulted together as to what was best to be done, and the latter, who had just crossed Yunnan so successfully, assured his companion that they need fear nothing; he had only recently been kindly received at both the towns mentioned above, and he proposed with his usual enterprising spirit that he should go on alone to test the accuracy of the various rumours afloat, promising to send back a messenger with news as soon as possible.

It was indeed unfortunate that the Colonel should have agreed to this rash suggestion, and allowed his unfortunate young colleague to go to his death. Little dreaming of the approaching tragedy, however, the two sat over their last meal together till far into the night, discussing the probable results of their expedition, regardless of the noise made by the beating of gongs and playing of cymbals to be heard from the pass, and of the fact that they could actually see the Kakhyens spying upon them from the lofty trees overlooking their camp.

At sunrise on the 19th Margary crossed the frontier, accompanied by his faithful secretary, the servants who had been with him since he left Shanghai, and a few Burmese muleteers. The next day Colonel Browne received a letter from him announcing his safe arrival at Seray, adding that he had been well received there, and was now on his way to Manwyne. The rest of the expedition followed in his footsteps, arriving at Seray on the 21st. No further news was received from Margary, but Colonel Browne was alarmed by rumours that he and his people were to be attacked, and by the fact that the chief mandarin of the place was arming his retainers. On the morning of the 22nd the storm burst, the Colonel's camp was surrounded by armed men, and at the same time letters were received from some Burmans residing at Manwyne telling of the cowardly assassination of Margary in that town.

But for the courage and steadfastness of his Burmese escort, especially of fifteen sepoys who formed a kind of body-guard, Colonel Browne would have shared the fate of his young fellow-countryman, but after a fierce struggle he succeeded in re-crossing the frontier with no worse casualties than three men wounded.

From Bhâmo every possible effort was made to ascertain the truth about the murder of Margary, but full details were never obtained. The most apparently trustworthy account was that given by a Burmese, who said he had seen the victim at Manwyne several times on the 21st, once alone and later walking with several Chinese. According to this witness, the young Englishman had been invited to ride out to see a spring of warm water, and that just as he issued from the town he was suddenly dispatched with their spears.

Thus apparently ended the attempt to open the land route between Burma and China, but as a matter of fact the death of Margary eventually did more for the interests of his country than the peaceful conclusion of Colonel Browne's expedition could ever have accomplished. The English know how to turn to account every incident, however tragic, however seemingly adverse to their own interests, and the indemnity wrung from the reluctant Chinese for the murder of the young Englishman included the opening of another 400 miles of the great river above Hankow, an immense step in advance towards the realization of the long-cherished British ambition; the connection of the Upper Yang-tze with Burma, so justly called England's land-gate to China. It is, in fact, in the provinces of Szechuan and Yunnan that the question of which European power is to have the supremacy in Central China will be finally fought out, and therefore every concession won in connection with them is alike of immense commercial and political significance.

CHAPTER VII

Sir Thomas Wade demands his passports—Retires to man-of-war off Tien-tsin—Interviews with Li-Hung-Chang—Convention of Che-Foo—Description of Ichang on the Yang-tse—The Manchester of Western China—Pak-hoï and its harbour—A magnificent pagoda—Ceremony of opening the port to foreign trade—New Year's *fête* at Pak-hoï—The game of Morra—Description of Wenchau—Temples and pagodas turned into inns—Wahn and its native officials—Dislike of mandarins, etc., to missionaries—Beautiful surroundings of the town—An eclipse of the moon expected—The eclipse does not keep time—Excitement of the people—The dragon attacks the moon at last—Threatening message from the Emperor to the astronomers—Two astronomers beheaded in B.C. 2155—Reasons for importance attached to eclipses in China.

NO good purpose would be served by relating in detail all the negotiations which took place after the death of Margary, between Sir Thomas Wade and the Government of Pekin, on the subject of the reparation to be made for the murder. It will be enough to say that after twenty months of shilly-shallying on the part of the Chinese and dogged perseverance on that of the British Envoy, the latter demanded his passports, shut up his legation with considerable *éclat*, and retired on board a man-of-war in the port of Tien-tsin, whence he issued a dignified threat of the imminent declaration of war between England and China if his demands were not complied with. This brought the Chinese Government to reason, for the Emperor and his advisers felt it would be better to yield everything than to see a victorious English army march a second time into Pekin. Sir Thomas Wade was therefore invited to meet the now celebrated Li-Hung-Chang, who became later so well-known in London and in Paris, at Che-Foo, a treaty port on the northern side of the province of Shantung, and there was signed the famous convention, of which on account of its great importance a *résumé* of the principal clauses is given here:

A large money indemnity, £60,000, was to be paid to the English Ambassador, to be distributed amongst the families of Europeans who should be in want or have lost their bread-winners in Yunnan. An Imperial edict would be sent to the Viceroy of Yunnan, who should discuss with some English official, a commercial treaty between Burma and the Chinese frontier province, where Margary met his fate. England was to have the right of appointing a representative at Tali-Fow, and he was to be seconded in his researches by the Chinese authorities; the country was to be opened to commerce; to avoid misunderstandings it would be for the Tsung-li-Yamen, or ministers of foreign affairs, to invite the various European legations to draw up and submit to them a code of etiquette by which alike the Chinese and foreign signatories to the agreement should be bound. China should send consuls and ambassadors to foreign countries; when a Chinese accused of a crime against a European is tried by the Chinese authorities, the European authorities shall have a right to be present in the court, but they must not interfere ; it is to be the same if the guilty person is a European who is tried by Englishmen. If, however, the representative of one of the two powers is not satisfied with the verdict given, he will have the right to protest. The penalty inflicted on the condemned will be that prescribed by the law of the country to which the judge belongs ; the *likin*, or inland tax, imposed on foreign goods in transit, is no longer to be exacted in the concessions belonging to Europeans ; China will permit Ichang in the province of Hupe, Wuhu in Anhui, Wenchow in Chekiang, and Pak-hoï in Canton to be opened to European trade ; consuls shall also be allowed to reside in each of these towns. Acting in a spirit of conciliation China will allow foreign steamers to take passengers and merchandise to the following ports on the Yang-tse : Ta-Tung, Anking, Hukow, Wusuch, Ling-hi-Kow, and Sha-Shi. Furthermore, if foreign expeditions wish to go by way of the Kansu and Kokonor route or by the way of Szechuan to Thibet and thence to India, the Tsung-li-Yamen will give the necessary passports to those expeditions, and instructions will also be sent to the Chinese officials of Thibet in order that the explorers may travel in all security.

This convention, which if fully acted on would have completely revolutionized the position of Europeans in China, was signed on the 13th September, 1876, but though more than twenty-

FIG. 36.—PORTRAIT CF HIS EXCELLENCY LI-HUNG-CHANG.

two years have passed since then, much of it still remains a dead letter. Now, however, there are many signs of the inauguration of a very different state of things; Chinese procrastinations and delays can no longer avert the final opening up of the whole country to European commerce and colonization, the only question being which of the

European powers will secure the largest share of the undeveloped wealth of the inland provinces.

It will be interesting before going further to inquire what is the present position of one or two of the ports mentioned in the *résumé* just given of the Treaty of 1876. We will begin with Ichang, recent events having brought it into considerable prominence. Beautifully situated on the banks of the Yang-tse, one thousand miles from its mouth, just at the entrance to the grand ravines of its middle course, great things were hoped of Ichang by the few Europeans who, emboldened by the delusive promises of the Chinese Government, took up their residence there in the early eighties. In 1883, we are told by Archibald Little, the intrepid English explorer, who last year took a specially-constructed steamer up to Chung-Ting, 500 miles beyond Ichang, "the foreign community in the latter town comprised a commissioner of customs with three assistants; one Scotch Presbyterian minister and his wife, and two Roman Catholic missionaries; whilst in 1898 the foreigners had increased to twelve Europeans employed in the Imperial customs, and thirty missionaries. The trade," he adds, "is a busy retail one, but there are no large banks or wealthy wholesale merchants such as there are at Sha-Shi, eighty miles lower down the river, which has been called the 'Manchester of Western China.' The opening to navigation of the Upper Yang-tse will doubtless ere long change all that, and the English owe a debt of gratitude to the pioneers who have broken through the long-sustained opposition of the junk-ring to the use of steamers. Ichang will, it is hoped, ere long become what its position marks it out to be—a centre of foreign trade for the long-closed border districts of Western China."

Pak-hoï, another of the Treaty ports of the 1876 Convention, presents a very marked contrast to Ichang. It is a town of some 10,000 inhabitants in the province of Canton, on the northern shore of Tonking, and is likely, now that the concession for the railway between it and Nanking has been secured by the French Government, to be of great importance as a port of export. Unfortunately, however, it has not a good harbour, and as at Hankow, large vessels are compelled to anchor in the offing on account of the lowness of the water further inshore. The chief imports to Pak-hoï are cotton and woollen goods, opium and rice, whilst the exports are sugar, ground-nut oil, aniseed, betel-vine leaves, and other spices. Lovers of sport will find plenty of woodcock, partridges, wild-ducks, and other water-fowl in the neighbourhood of Pak-hoï. Opposite to the town, in the south of the bay, is a very celebrated pagoda, one of the most remarkable in China. From its centre grows a magnificent plane-tree, in which nest thousands of sparrows. The branches have forced their way through the windows of the building, and the masses of dark green foliage, contrasting as they do with the stonework, produce a most charming and picturesque effect. The bay on which Pak-hoï is situated is dotted with islands, and in them many French missionaries have taken up their abode, adopting the costumes and many of the customs of the natives, including the wearing of the pig-tail. One of these devoted soldiers of the Cross had been an exile from his native land for nineteen years.

FIG. 37.—ICHANG.

Pak-hoï was opened to trade with considerable ceremony in the presence of the English Consul and several mandarins of high standing. The foreign flags were saluted by the Chinese with a volley from two guns, and the director of the new Custom House let off a number of crackers amongst the assembled crowds with a view to warning off evil spirits, who, in the opinion of the Celestials, are afraid of them. In spite of the expenditure of gunpowder, the receipts of the Pak-hoï Customs officers have so far remained insignificant, though there is every probability of a considerable increase in the near future.

It so happened that when I visited the town the *fête* of the New Year was being celebrated, which prevented my giving as much attention as I might otherwise have done to the statistics of trade. The year begins in China fifteen days after the rising of the February moon, and at this *fête* the Celestials, who are generally so devoted to business, throw aside all occupation and give themselves completely up to amusement. There is no Sabbath or weekly day of rest in this land of the yellow races, which perhaps accounts for the intense zest with which they enjoy the annual fortnight of repose.

On the eve of the holiday the Chinese merchant puts his business affairs into scrupulous order, balancing his accounts as he sits at his desk, bending over his numerous little ledgers, or his calculator made of tiny balls of ivory, his big spectacles upon his nose, and a pencil or a reed pen in his hand. His work done, he locks up his books and hastens off to don his very best clothes; then holding fast the indispensable fan, he runs off to the theatres and the flower-boats, treats his friends and becomes intoxicated as they do with opium, or with champagne, to the deafening accompaniment of the beating of gongs, or the explosion of thousands of crackers. Or if he is fonder of play than of drinking, he goes to some sordid gambling-den and there in a few hours dissipates the results of a whole year of toil. As in France at the beginning of a new year many presents are exchanged by the Celestials, and a well-brought-up Chinaman sends to each of his friends a little square piece of red paper on which, side by side with the name of the donor, is inscribed some wise precept of Confucius.

FIG. 38.—A CHINESE DYER AT WORK.

To the women with whom he is on visiting terms he will present small lacquer articles, microscopic shrubs, or quaint representations of fish with red scales and golden fins. If he is anxious to secure the patronage of some merchant or trader, he will send him beautiful fruit, such as Mandarin oranges, dainty hams, or sugar-candy, according to what he knows to be the recipient's special weakness.

At the *fête* of the New Year the wives of the mandarins and other officials exchange visits in their ornate palanquins, dressed up in their finest silk dresses, generally either yellow or blue, and with their faces laden with rouge. Endless is the talk these decked-out dames have together, as they sip their tea from tiny little cups, and nibble sweets, or munch up immense quantities of dried and strongly-salted slices of water-melon. At these feminine re-unions, too, there is a good deal of singing, and the voices are pitched so high that a stranger passing by a house where a concert was going on would think a lot of amorous cats were yelling on the roof.

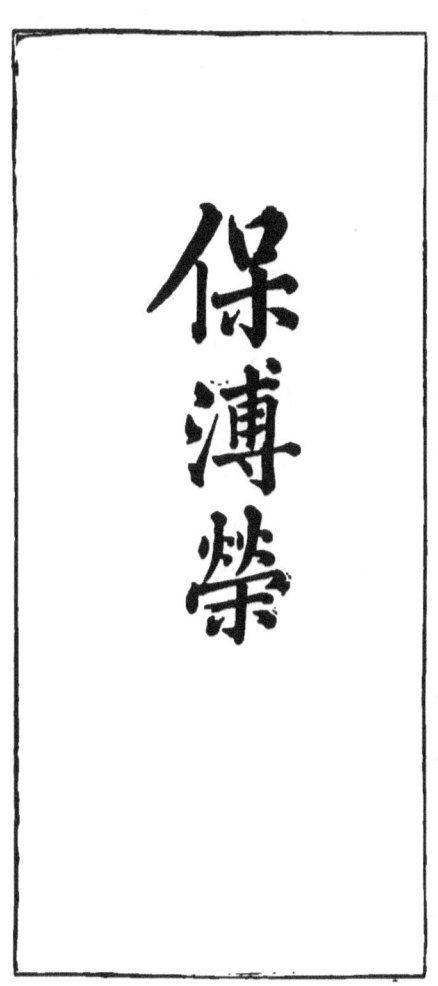

FIG. 39.—A CHINESE VISITING CARD.

None of the lower classes will do any work on a general holiday, and the coolies, palanquin-bearers, and boatmen, who have not much money to risk, content themselves with playing at the popular and almost cosmopolitan game of morra at the street-corners, shouting and laughing over it with wonderful animation, forty Celestials making more noise than would five hundred Europeans. Sometimes the game ends in a quarrel, but even when he is insulted a Chinaman never fights; his mode of working off his spleen is quite unlike that of the corresponding class in the West.

Wenchow is an important town on the coast of the fertile and beautifully-wooded province of Chekiang, and is about equi-distant from Fuchau and Tsing-Ho. It is the port of embarkation for great quantities of tea, and considerable trade is done in it in bamboo, wood, and timber. It is a bright, clean-looking town, as well kept as any in the Flowery Land, as Chinese authors love to call their country, and the streets are said by travellers to be wider than those of any other city of the Celestial Empire. There are, moreover, such an immense number of temples, that inns being scarce, Europeans often lodge in the sacred buildings, the natives offering no objection; but it must be added that in many parts of China, pagodas are turned to account as caravanserais in which any one is allowed to sleep and to cook food. In spite of all the stories told of the bigotry of the Chinese, and of the awful penalties exacted for sacrilege, there is really no doubt that taken as a whole the inhabitants of the Celestial Empire are really less intolerant than those of Europe, a fact which should not be forgotten in passing judgment upon them. The port of Wenchow has increased rapidly in prosperity since the Convention of 1876 threw it open to European trade, and many foreign vessels are always in the harbour, discharging their cargoes of various stuffs, or taking Chinese merchandise on board.

Wu-hu, fifty miles from Nanking, is on the Yang-tse, and so far has not profited very much by its new privileges, though it now seems likely to become a centre of the rice-exporting trade of the surrounding districts. The story goes that the first Englishman to settle in Wu-hu wrote to a fellow-countryman at Shanghai soon after his arrival, to say he had drunk so much champagne with the Chinese governor that he was quite unable to describe his new quarters. He had arrived in a snow-storm, a happy augury according to the natives, but far from a pleasant one to a European. Wu-hu is the residence of a civil magistrate, and of a *tao-tai*, whose duties are very much those of a Prefect in French towns. There are also a colonel, who has two regiments of soldiers under him, and two naval officers in the Imperial service. One of the latter is in command of the fleet stationed at the mouth of the Yang-tse, the other looks after the gun-boats which act as the river police. The town is well built, the chief street is a league long, well paved and bordered by beautiful houses, some two storeys high, and all decorated with red or black lacquer signs on which stand out the names in golden letters of the merchants owning them. When this fine street is lit up by the oblique rays of the setting sun the effect is as dazzling as at Canton itself. The climate is healthy, the people are friendly to foreigners, so that many causes combine to make Wu-hu a pleasant place of residence for Europeans. It must, however, be added that the mandarins and government officials are alike hostile to missionaries.

On every side of the town, except of course on that of the river, stretch vast plantations of rice and corn-fields. A raised causeway crosses these beautiful and well-kept districts, along which I went with a fellow-countryman, a French naval officer, to be present at a noisy demonstration by the natives in honour of an eclipse of the moon. On this occasion, however, the satellite of our earth so much beloved by poets played the astronomers of Pekin a very scurvy trick.

The learned members of the Kin-Tien-Kien, or Imperial astronomers, had with all due solemnity announced to the Emperor of China, the Son of Heaven, as well as to all the provincial governors, that on the 7th February at eight o'clock in the evening precisely, the dragon who wanders to and fro in the regions of the air, *quærens quem devoret*, will endeavour to swallow the moon. The eclipse was to be almost total, so the astronomers had warned the people that the attack of the monster would be terrible, and that the pale satellite of the earth would very likely succumb if the shouts and the noise of the gongs did not put the dragon to flight.

Long before the appointed time on the day when the tragedy was expected to come off, millions of Chinese issued from all the towns of the vast Empire to flock out into the open country, there, nose in air, to watch the wonderful phenomenon about, as they supposed, to take place. Those amongst them who had been unable to get gongs, had provided themselves with saucepans, rattles, pieces of the hollow stems of the bamboo, and immense quantities of little red crackers. But, oh, what a disappointment! Oh, what a fraud! At eight o'clock the gazing multitudes saw the moon rise above the horizon in all the untarnished glory of her full disc, without the slightest sign of any alteration in her usual appearance. At nine o'clock she was shining placidly down upon the watchers, her radiance totally unimpaired. Was the whole thing a mystification, a fabrication of the astronomers? But just as all hope was being regretfully abandoned, a tremendous noise began on every side, for the watchers saw a change coming over the face of the planet, which was assuming a reddish hue like that of blood, whilst a hideous black spot was slowly advancing across it. The dragon was beginning his attack.

It is absolutely impossible to describe the rage with which the Chinese then began to beat their gongs and saucepans, whirl their rattles, and let off their crackers. The dragon was evidently frightened away by the row, for after an hour of looking up at the full moon, and seeing nothing more of the black spot, the crowds, jubilant over their action, began to disperse, whilst the planet triumphantly continued her course through space.

I learnt later that the Emperor sent a message to his astronomers telling them that next time they made such a mistake in their calculations he would relieve them of their appointments and send them into exile. In the reign of Tchung Kang, 2155 years before the Christian era, his astronomers named Hi and Ho were beheaded for not having foreseen an eclipse of the sun. Father Gaubil, in his interesting *History of Chinese Astronomy*, explains the reasons of this very severe punishment as follows :

"In China an eclipse of the sun or of the moon is considered of evil augury for the Emperor, intended to warn him to examine himself and correct his faults. . . . Hence an eclipse is always looked upon as an affair of state in the Celestial Empire, and the greatest care is taken to calculate the time when one will take place, as well as to observe it whilst it is going on with the ceremonies prescribed on such occasions. Now this time Hi and Ho had failed altogether to announce the approaching event, and when the orb of day was suddenly obscured, the mandarins, not expecting an eclipse, hastened to the palace in alarmed dismay. The confusion which ensued of course terrified the people, who had also been left in ignorance of the approaching phenomenon. The whole course of the proper proceedings on these occasions is presented in the ancient book of rites. Directly the light of the sun begins to grow dim, the chief musician strikes a drum, and the mandarins are all expected to hurry at once to the palace armed with bows and arrows, as if to aid the Emperor, who is supposed to be the image of the sun. All the officials, moreover, have to offer their sovereign pieces of silk. Meanwhile the Emperor and the chief dignitaries of the court don their simplest garments and fast. As the astronomers did not give the usual notice, all these ceremonies, generally so religiously observed, were neglected, and, although Hi and Ho were princes as well as men of science, they had to pay the penalty of their neglect. They were not at court at the time, but at their country seats, where, said Rumour, they were conspiring against their sovereign. They were arrested, and without any trial the Emperor ordered their heads to be cut off. Thus dramatically ended an episode thoroughly characteristic of the Celestial Empire, where the Son of Heaven has ever been ready to order those who annoy him on earth to be decapitated, inquiring into their conduct only when the proving of their innocence can do them no good.

CHAPTER VIII

I land at Shanghai—The Celestial who had never heard of Napoleon—Total value of exports and imports to and from Shanghai—What those exports and imports are—The devotion of the Chinese to their native land—The true yellow danger of the future—I am invited to a Chinese dinner at Shanghai—My yellow guests—The ladies find me amusing—Their small feet and difficulty in walking—A wealthy mandarin explains why the feet are mutilated—Sale of girls in China—Position of women discussed—A mandarin accepts a Bible—Our host takes us to a flower-boat—Description of boat—My first attempt at opium-smoking—A Celestial in an opium dream.

WHEN I landed on the vast estuary from which rises up the important town of Shanghai, I really could hardly believe I was but forty days' voyage from Marseilles. Our world is no such big one after all, it is true, but how many centuries it has taken to learn much about it! "Did you ever hear of Napoleon?" I one day asked a Celestial, who had a shining glass button on his cap. "Don't know whom you mean," he answered, with a bewildered look, and there is not much doubt that if he had asked me about some great Chinese Emperor, I should have been just as puzzled as he was. All this will, however, ere long be changed, what with steam and electricity, especially with electricity, which puts a girdle round the earth in a very few minutes, fleet messenger that it is of peace, of war, of ruin, and of fortune. When the various races of the earth know each other better, we shall perhaps become more tolerant of each other, more interdependent, so to speak, and that cannot fail to be an advantage for all concerned. When a blow struck in the East is enough to shake the West to its foundations, we shall think twice before we give that blow. The more frequent the intercourse between the various races of the earth, the nearer we shall be, in spite of many a bitter disappointment, to that era of universal peace to which every nation has aspired in vain for so many centuries.

Such were some of my reflections when I found myself for the first time in the midst of the busy scenes on the quays of Shanghai, surrounded by countless bales of silk and cases of tea waiting for embarkation for the West from whence I came. Shanghai, as is well known, is the port of entry of that great water highway of Western China, the Yang-tse, but it is more than that, it is the commercial capital of the Celestial Empire, for, as stated by Colquhoun in his *China in Transformation*, fifty-five per cent. of the total value of the foreign imports at all the treaty ports, and forty-eight per cent. of the exports to foreign countries pass through the port of Shanghai. " Four years ago the value of the trade, native and foreign, of this great emporium of the East was estimated at no less than £35,772,006, and it has increased rather than decreased since then. Several steamers have plied daily since 1860 between Shanghai and Hankow, and some three thousand vessels, one-half of which are British, enter the port every year. Silk and tea are the chief exports, after which come cotton, rice, sugar, paper, tobacco, various drugs used as medicines, cloth of native manufacture, wool, hemp, flower-seeds, fans, and other fancy articles." The chief imports from abroad are cotton goods, alcohol, opium, which is fortunately rapidly declining in amount, various metals, and woollen stuffs. In 1896, France, whose trade with China takes third rank amongst that of European nations, England coming first and then Germany, exported goods to the value of one hundred and eighty-four millions of francs, on which she paid one million five hundred thousand francs duty. To set against this, French imports to China, including woven materials, lace, wine, copper, and other goods, amounted to the value of twenty-eight millions only; that is to say, one hundred and fifty-six millions less than the exports. What an immense difference does this sum represent between what China gave and what she received, and what a price the Chinese paid for the privilege of dealing with the West! To this day the Celestials, whose ports have been opened against their will by the cannon of the British, aided by those of the

French, give what they must give to foreigners grudgingly; to use an expressive saying, there is no love lost between them and those they trade with. They would like to take all and give nothing in return. Those who are unfortunate enough to die abroad will not allow their dust to aid in fructifying the soil of the land of their exile, for their bodies are brought by steamers from San Francisco, Peru, the Philippine Islands, Australia, and elsewhere, to be buried in their native land, in the same last resting-place as that of their ancestors, where their memory will be held sacred by their own descendants. There is indeed something very pathetic and touching in the intense devotion of the Chinese to their native land, in spite of their ignorant readiness to leave it. They will make any sacrifice to ensure burial at home, for they believe that there alone can the dead find true repose.

When I was at Shanghai, I noted with some surprise what immense quantities of bales of cotton were landed at the port. An Englishman with whom I had some conversation told me these bales came from the East Indies, and that the amount imported was continually on the increase. The Chinese aspire, he added, to manufacturing cotton goods themselves, and if they should succeed in overcoming their aversion to European methods of production, the trade in stuffs will receive a severe blow. It is, however, greatly in favour of British manufacturing interests that

Western China is not suitable to the cultivation of the raw material, so that the cotton for making much of the clothing of the natives has all to be brought from abroad. "Every traveller in the Upper Yang-tse," says Little in his *Through the Yang-tse Gorges*, "is struck by the endless procession of cotton-laden junks struggling up the successive rapids."

A more significant sign of the times and of the emancipation of many of the Chinese from the trammels of tradition, even than the desire to produce their clothes at home, is the willingness of traders and merchants to settle in foreign towns. Not so very long ago the only Chinese met with in Europe or America were the coolies who had emigrated on the conditions described in a previous chapter. Now in London, in Paris, and in New York are extensive depôts of tea, silk, and other exports from the Celestial Empire kept by Chinese men of wealth, with a staff of their own yellow countrymen. This fact represents the true yellow peril for European and American merchants, for these merchants sell better goods at lower prices than their foreign rivals, and the employers of labour will presently have to contend in their own persons with a competition as keen and as unequal as that hampering their workmen. The fact that the Chinese will work for very much lower wages than those on which any white man can support life, has long been a problem for those responsible for municipal government in the States, but it is only

FIG. 40.—A CHINESE RESTAURANT. AFTER THE REPAST.

AN INVITATION TO DINNER

lately that the monied classes have been, so to speak, threatened with a similar danger in their own strongholds of trade and commerce. If restrictions are not soon imposed upon the entry into Paris and other great cities of Europe of these formidable rivals, we may yet in our own lifetime see the yellow-skins driven through the streets before the bayonet and the revolver in our capitals, in much the same fashion as they already have been in California and Australia. But when all is said and done, have not Asiatics just as much right to rejoice in the sunshine, such as it is, of the West as Europeans have to bask in that of the East? Is not the life of a Tartar, a Mongol, or a Mandarin really as sacred as that of a native of France or of England? It all depends on the point of view.

A wealthy American, who had been longer at Shanghai than any other foreigner, invited me to dine with him at a celebrated Chinese restaurant, and there I enjoyed the rare privilege of meeting several natives of high rank. They came accompanied by their favourite concubines, their legal wives being left at home; and the ladies were carried in their palanquins right into the centre of the dining-room, where they got out. Dressed in fresh and elegant costumes of light blue silk, and with their abundant black hair decked with natural flowers, they really looked very pretty. Their complexions, though far too much rouged, were delicate; and where the natural hue had been left unchanged, almost white. Sitting at table with them, I regretted very much that I could not say a word they would understand, for they spoke neither French nor English, and I do not understand Chinese. My host had, however, warned me to be very careful not to be too polite to them even in dumb-show, for if their lords felt the very smallest spark of jealousy I should most likely see all the fair creatures take flight like a flock of frightened turtle-doves. Their palanquins were waiting outside at the door of the restaurant, ready for every contingency. The Celestials invited had only consented to come to this dinner when they were assured that I should be leaving Shanghai in a few days. Throughout the meal the women talked very little amongst themselves, but I saw a smile of amusement on their lips when they noticed my embarrassment at having to take something to which I was not accustomed; such as pigeons' hearts with ginger, to drink spirit distilled from rice out of little cups instead of glasses, and to pick up my food with the ivory chop-sticks, which did duty for forks. None of the ladies ate any meat, and they put nothing into their dainty mouths but perfumed sweets or dried melon-seeds, which they picked up with their long, slim fingers, disfigured by great claw-like nails, giving their hands a very unpleasant, almost bestial appearance. The meal consisted of three courses, during the serving of which vocal and instrumental music—oh, such a lot of it!—was going on. When it was over, the young women rose, and, still smiling, made their way out with difficulty on their poor deformed feet, clutching at the table, the chairs, and the walls for support as they limped to their luxurious palanquins. The last to leave had feet so tiny I could hardly see them beneath her jonquil-coloured silk breeches. I remarked on the small size of the poor girl's feet to a corpulent Celestial with an intelligent face who was sitting beside me, and he said with a loud laugh, "Very good thing for jealous husbands!"

"Small feet are not merely a caprice of fashion then?" I observed.

"No, no!" was the reply. "The fact is, when in any family, whether rich or poor, a girl-child is born, who is well formed and has good features, giving great promise of beauty when she is fifteen years old, her feet are subjected to close compression a few months after birth. You will understand that it is her liberty to walk or run, and to get out of the house, which is taken away from her at this early stage of her existence. . . . Later, when her parents, if wealthy, wish to find a good match for her, or if poor are anxious to sell her for a high price, her small feet are always quoted as a proof of her value, and this privation of liberty is considered a great point in her favour . . . do you see?"

"What a barbarous custom!" I exclaimed.

"Yes, from the European point of view, but if you had asked any of the girls who were at dinner just now, whether Hatai, Atma, Atoi, or Atchai, each one would have replied that she did not regret the life that she leads. If she had not been prepared in this way to be bought by some wealthy Celestial, she would have been working in the rice-plantations like a beast of burden; or would have had to spend her life with the fisher-folk on the sea-shore, or in some wretched river-boat."

"How are these sales of women effected?" I inquired.

"Through the agency of brokers, and by formal contract. At this moment I have a document in my pocket making me the owner from to-day of a young girl of Tien-tsin. Would you like to see it?"

Of course I said yes, and he showed me the contract, of which I give a verbatim translation:

"On account of the poverty of my family, I consent to sell my daughter, aged fourteen years, to Tu-won-lan-hi, that he may provide for and take care of her. On the twenty-fourth day of the sixth moon, I received as complete payment for her the sum of eighty-five piastres (about six pounds). The twenty-fourth day of the sixth month of the sixteenth year of the reign of Kwang-Su.[1]

"*Signed:* THANG TING, father of the young girl;
"Madame YAP-KANG-KO, go-between;
"TCHEN-TCHEN-TCHAN, scribe charged with drawing up the contract of sale."

[1] In China, the year of the reign is used instead of that of the century, and a century there is only sixty years. According to Chinese chronology, we are now in the thirty-fifth year of the seventy-sixth century of the Christian era.

Having read and copied this document, I returned it to the owner, with the remark, "So you can have as many women as it suits you to buy. In Egypt, where polygamy seems as natural as it does to you, there is some limit put upon the number of favourites in a harem, as the purchaser must prove that he is rich enough to support her before he is allowed to buy a new wife. How is it with you?"

"There is no similar restriction in China," was the reply. "Besides the women we buy, more as a gratification to our pride than because we have taken a fancy to them, there is the wife whom you in Europe would call the legitimate partner. She is privileged above all the other women owned by a man, and her children alone have the right of inheriting the property of their father. We must have heirs to succeed us, and this is why we have no scruple in repudiating a barren wife. The first of our other women to give us a male child takes the place of the divorced wife, and the rest follow suit, until we are sure of having quite a number of sons to honour our memories when we are gone, just as I have honoured that of my own father. You must not forget how very strong tradition is with us, and that which we are now discussing dates further back than your own Biblical age. All innovation is displeasing to us. . . . A few years ago the friend who gave us a dinner this evening, put me into communication with a Protestant clergyman, who had just arrived from

England, and was consumed with a desire to make proselytes. Out of politeness, I listened for several days to what he had to say, and I even accepted the gift of a Bible from him. I set to work to read it with the greatest attention. To begin with, I was very much surprised to find how young the world was made out to be in it, for I had learnt from our bonzes that at the time when Abraham was born, China was already old—very, very old—so I put the Bible aside. Was I not right, seeing that it taught me nothing new?"

"No," I replied, "you should have read on till you came to the New Testament, for in it you would have found that man is not meant to live in a state of debasing immobility, and that woman has a very different mission to fulfil than that of the mere beast of burden, or concubine you make of her in China."

Fortunately, perhaps, for the conversation was becoming rather acrimonious, our host interrupted us by inviting us to go with him to a *fête* which was being given in the harbour by a mandarin friend of his, a great opium-smoker, and owner of what in the Celestial Empire by a chivalrous euphemism is called a "Flower Boat."

A few vigorous strokes from the oars of our boatmen brought us alongside a junk riding at anchor in the open roadstead of Shanghai. The interior, draped with scarlet damask, was brilliantly illuminated by means of an immense number of dainty little lanterns, beneath which hung cages filled with birds, whilst other cages upheld glass globes where red fish, with long golden tails and transparent fins, disported themselves, their size fantastically exaggerated by the medium through which we watched their graceful movements. Very finely-woven mats of gleaming cleanliness covered the floors, and curtains of embroidered silk slightly raised hung at the entrances to the cabins, half concealing, half revealing, the mysterious recesses within. I went into one of these retreats, and there in the centre of the room I saw seated round a table, loaded with flowers, a number of pale-faced Chinamen, each with a fan in his hand, with several richly-dressed women (all, as usual, too much rouged), who were sipping tea together or nibbling sweetmeats to the accompaniment of a guitar. I noted also a couch of satin, without mattress or palliasse, but with a pillow consisting of a cylinder of red chequered cardboard, and not far from the couch a fragile bamboo table, on which were placed a metal pipe, a box of opium, and the little lamps indispensable to the smokers of the drug.

I was presented to the mandarin, who was giving the entertainment, and found him to be a man of very dignified appearance. He had lived for a long time at Hong-Kong, and spoke a little English. He was very anxious to perform his duties of host properly with regard to me, but did not find it very easy.

"What will you take?" he and the gentleman who had brought me kept saying one after the other.

A queer fancy took possession of me all of a sudden, and I replied that I should like to smoke some opium.

"Well, then," was the answer, "will you go into that cabin?" He clapped his hands, and a servant ran in to light the lamps.

When this was done, my host said: "I will send you a little tea as well, in case the opium should not suit you. I suppose it is the first time you have ever smoked it."

The tea was placed ready to my hand, and I was left alone, the curtain falling as the servant retired. I then smoked my first pipe, and found the flavour of it detestably nasty. I now stretched myself in the couch, laid my head upon the hard glazed roll of cardboard, which did duty as a pillow, and closed my eyes. After a few minutes of anything but pleasant meditation, I suddenly felt very unwell, and looked about me distractedly. Seeing a porthole close to me, I put my head through it, hoping that the fresh air would cool my burning forehead, but the sight of the black water of the harbour, and the dreary sound of its surging up and down, made me worse, so I quickly drew back and lay down again, determined to persevere. At the end of a quarter of an hour I had smoked two more pipes, and then I issued from my cabin with a very vague idea about my own sensations, but feeling like a man suddenly overtaken by giddiness, or seized with violent sea-sickness.

My Yankee friend hastened to my assistance,

but before he saw me off the boat, he took me to have a look at the stout Chinaman with whom I had had a discussion about the Bible. He was alone in a smoking-den, just like the one I had used. His face was ghastly pale, his eyes were widely distended, and he was gazing at the waves with an expression of terror, whilst his features were bathed in perspiration. . . . He was wrapt in a dream—a happy dream, no doubt—though his looks belied it, for surely so many Asiatics would not smoke the opium which brings the dreams if they were not happy!

FIG. 41.—A CHINESE JUNK.

CHAPTER IX

Great commercial value of opium—Cultivation of the poppy—Exports of opium from India—What opium is—Preparation of the drug—Opinions on the English monopoly of the trade in it—Ingenious mode of smuggling opium—Efforts of Chinese Government to check its importation—Proclamation of the Viceroy Wang—Opinion of Li-Shi-Shen on the properties of opium—The worst form of opium smoking—Its introduction to Formosa by the Dutch—Depopulation of the island—Punishments inflicted on opium-smokers—Opinions of doctors on the effects of opium-eating or smoking—Chinese prisoners deprived of their usual pipe—The real danger to the poor of indulgence in opium—Evidence of Archibald Little—The Chinese and European pipe contrasted.

OPIUM has from the first been so important a factor in the history of Western intercourse with China, and indulgence in it is said to have had so much to do with the physical and mental inferiority of the modern Celestials, that it will be well to devote a chapter to the consideration of the nature of the drug and its effects.

The poppy (*papaver somniferum*), from which the narcotic is extracted, is grown in Persia and in China, but it is in India that it is most largely and successfully cultivated. The monopoly of producing it in her great Eastern dependency, and of selling it to the Chinese, has always been vigorously protected by England, and the destruction of that monopoly when it comes will be an immense loss to the revenue. Opium is, in fact, to the English what tobacco is to the French, and there is no doubt that British missionary effort has been greatly hampered by the dread of the authorities of any interference with their lucrative trade.

In the vast and fertile valley of the Ganges, the poppy has but to be sown to yield an extensive crop. The Patna and Benares districts are especially prolific, and at the time of efflorescence the air is laden with the heavy, enervating scent from the flowers. Nothing could be much more dreary and monotonous than the appearance of an Indian poppy plantation, when the soil is covered with the dried petals of the flower. Some few years ago the tax on the exported drug, both from Calcutta and from Bombay, amounted to considerably over six millions of pounds. The cultivators take their produce to the Government factories, where it is purchased from them, and then sent to the sea-port, so that any illicit consumption is rendered almost impossible. The comparatively small amount of opium consumed in India itself is taxed by the excise officers, and the bulk of the crop finds its way to China. It is only of late years that native opium has competed at all with Indian, but already it is rumoured that eventually it will drive the foreign imports away altogether. Szechnan opium is taking the place of Indian on the Yang-tse, and Little, in his *Through the Yang-tse Gorges*, describes vast poppy plantations in the districts watered by the great river. He bemoans the association of the English name "with the introduction of the useful yet pernicious drug," and points out that it was first brought to China from India by the Portuguese, adding that, in any case, the opium-pipe is most surely a Chinese invention, for it is unknown in any other land.

Opium in its first state is the dried juice of the capsules before they are ripe, and is gathered in the form of little globules of milky sap, of the colour of amber. In India the seed is sown early in November, and the capsules are ready for piercing about the beginning of February, when they are nearly as large as hen's eggs. The delicate operation of opening the poppy-heads for the exudation of the precious fluid is performed with an instrument about three inches long, consisting of four small knives bound together, the edges looking like the teeth of a comb. The labourers have each several of these instruments, which, when not in use, they carry carefully in a case. The day after the capsules have been pierced, the juice is collected by scraping it off into a kind of scoop, or small trowel, whence it is transferred to an earthen pot, hanging from the collector's side When full, these pots are carefully covered over and carried to the gatherer's home. The contents of the jar require the most careful attention for three or four weeks to ensure proper and equal drying. The juice is poured into a shallow plate or dish of brass, slightly tilted, to let any watery fluid, which would spoil the drug, drain off, and when the process is complete, the opium is carefully packed in jars of equal size, and taken to the Government factories. Here it is carefully examined, chemically tested, and weighed, to make sure that it has not been tampered with in any way; and, if all is well, it is placed in pots of the regulation size: the pots are ticketed and ranged in rows on shelves in a big room set apart for the purpose. The rest of the preparation for export is done in the Government laboratories, and the process is a long and delicate one. The united crops of vast districts are thrown into large tubs, where they are kneaded up together till they are of the right consistency. The material is then taken out, divided into equal portions, and placed on small tables, where it is manipulated, with the aid of copper bowls of a spherical shape, into balls of an equal weight, of about the size of a man's head. Some workmen become so skilful that they turn out a hundred of these balls a day. Poppy-leaves, reduced to powder, are used to prevent the opium from sticking together, and the balls are sprinkled with the powder, much as chemists used to sprinkle pills.

The opium thus prepared, is now placed in great

earthenware pans, and carried to a drying-room, where the balls are ranged in rows of mathematical regularity. During the drying process each sphere is pierced every now and then with a long needle, to prevent the fermentation, which, but for the greatest vigilance, might set in. The pricking also sets free the gas which would rapidly deteriorate the value of the drug, prevents it from becoming musty, and drives off the swarms of insects attracted by the smell from it.

The cases in which the balls of opium are packed are made of wood from the mountains of Nepaul, which is brought to its destination in the form of huge rafts. These rafts come down the Ganges on sailing vessels, at the approach of which all other crafts have to make way. Calcutta is the port of export for Bengal, and the opium is shipped into steamers and taken to Hong-Kong or Shanghai.

As is well known, the British Government has been very severely criticized, not only by foreigners, but by English philanthropists, for maintaining the opium monopoly, and the entire cessation of the trade from India is earnestly advocated. Those who wish to maintain things as they are, urge that the control exercised by the authorities is a beneficent one, and that but for it opium would be cultivated throughout the whole of India, and its consumption increased a thousand-fold. Time, the great equalizer, will no doubt in the end keep up the monopoly without any definite action on the part of the English, for although nominally forbidden, the culture of the poppy is encouraged in China by the officials responsible for the enforcement of the law, and immense quantities of opium of native production is sold in the western provinces, for a much lower price than the imported drug.

The opium of Bengal is still preferred by critical smokers, but that of Smyrna is more largely used in medicine, for it contains a greater proportion of morphine, and is sent in large quantities to England, and to Belgium. The culture of the poppy has of late years also been tried in Africa, Australia, and even in parts of America, but so far the opium produced in those countries does not compete with the Asiatic to any perceptible degree.

As a very little opium represents a considerable money value, smuggling is of course practised on a very large scale, especially in China, where the ingenuity displayed is really extraordinary. All along the coast, and that coast is of immense extent, the illicit trade is briskly carried on. In the South the smuggled drug is brought in in very fleet vessels, of light tonnage, which easily evade the boats of the revenue officers. The steamers plying daily between the open ports of Hong-Kong and Canton do much to help the traffic, for the Celestials, who take passage on them, secrete the precious drug about their own persons in a manner most difficult to detect. Quantities of opium are also often hidden beneath sham planks, in the paddles of the wheels, in the pipes of the fire-engines, and even in the clocks on board. The struggle between the smugglers and the custom-house officers is never-ending, and the skill displayed in concealment on the one side and detection on the other is so nearly equal, that it is rare indeed for either to gain a decisive victory over the other.

There is something truly pathetic in the futile efforts made at various times by the Chinese Government to prevent the importation of opium into the country, and of the many viceroys of provinces to keep it out of the districts under their care. Here is a typical proclamation, issued by a certain Wang in the early days of the trade in the pernicious drug, which gives a very fair idea of what may be called native administrative literature:

"Wang, Imperial Viceroy, makes known the following: Advices have reached us to the effect that in the capital of Kwang-Tung and the neighbouring districts certain E-jen (barbarians from the West) are going about distributing to the people drugs in the form of pills made by fairies and evil genii. It is asserted that those who have absorbed these drugs sweat terribly all over their bodies to such an extent that they die.

" I order all civil and military authorities to seek out the distributors of these diabolical medicines, to arrest them, and to bring them to the Court of Justice, where I will punish them severely. Although there are no proofs that in my own district the E-jen have ventured to sell the pills in question, I have been assured that cakes injurious to health have been distributed to the people. Analyzed with the aid of white of egg, these cakes yielded a residue of maggots. . . . I immediately ordered the arrest of the presumptuous merchants, but they had already fled beyond my jurisdiction. Fifty strokes from a bamboo-rod on the soles of their feet would have been their punishment. The fact is, I am very much afraid that these wretches have gone to other provinces, there to carry on their trade and do further mischief.

"From another report I learn that every day certain E-jen throw deadly poisonous powders upon the roads; the rain does not destroy their potency for evil; when these powders are trodden under foot a thin, suffocating smoke rises up from them; there are some E-jen who carry this pernicious substance at the end of their fingers, and they have but to rub the head of any one they meet with it for that person to die, his body becoming covered with red spots.

"Have a care, therefore, not to allow yourselves to be duped; I give you notice that at the gates of the town in which I reside I have posted policemen who examine all strangers."

In 1578 the celebrated Chinese savant, Li-Shi-Shen, published his great book on the materials employed in medicine, to which he had devoted his whole life. In this book he gives the history of the poppy and its cultivation, dividing that history into three parts, the first relating to the early days when its properties were little known, that is to say, from the eighth to the eleventh century; the second to the time when the juice of the capsules was discovered to have medicinal properties and became used to alleviate affections of the stomach; and the third when opium was imported in solid form. Li-Shi-Shen justly remarks that it is in the capsule or seed-pod that the opium juice is secreted, and he recommends the use of that juice mixed with honey for certain maladies. He makes fun of a doctor who lived before his time, and had said that the juice of the poppy could kill as surely as a stroke from a sword, but dwells on the immense relief which those suffering from rheumatism and asthma had obtained from its use. This sage of the sixteenth century adds, that in Pekin opium pills are used to arouse sexual passion. There is nothing surprising in this assertion to those who know the Chinese and their fondness for such queer diet as swallows' nests, ginger, the fins of sharks, sea-urchins, etc., because they think they stimulate the senses. It must, however, be added in justice to the Celestials, that they are far less sensual than their neighbours, the Japanese, and this is no small praise.

Though Li-Shi-Shen was right in laughing at the doctor whose assertion is quoted above, the abuse of the newly-discovered drug of opium did cause a great many deaths, and in the seventeenth century many Imperial edicts were issued forbidding its use, but so deeply rooted had the love of it become, that these fulminations against it were powerless to prevent its importation. The mortality was doubled when the Chinese learnt to mix opium with Hashish, or the potent drug known in India as bhang, prepared from hemp.

The fatal knowledge was imparted to the Celestials in 1625 by some Batavians who had come to Formosa, then in the possession of the Dutch, who were engaged in building Fort Zealandia, near the present Taiwan. The pernicious compound is smoked through a pipe fixed on to a bamboo handle, and those who indulge in it are thrown into a state of delirium, which generally lasts for a whole night. The results in the island of Formosa were immediate and tragic, for all who had once enjoyed the voluptuous dreams induced by the double narcotic, conceived such a passion for the poison that no restrictive measures had any effect. The Dutch, alarmed at the rapid depopulation of the island, did their best to remedy the evil, but it was all of no use, the union of opium and Hashish was more devastating than an epidemic of cholera or small-pox would have been. If a native were condemned to the bastinado he would beg to be allowed to smoke his pipe whilst the punishment was being inflicted, and the blows from the bamboo fell all unheeded on his shoulders. According to some accounts it was this demoralization of the natives which led the Dutch to abandon Formosa, whilst others say they were driven out in 1866 by the Chinese. In any case it seems pretty certain that the worst form of opium smoking began during the Dutch occupation of Formosa, and was thence introduced to the mainland. It is consoling to know that Chinese historians attribute to the Dutch, not the English, the introduction of the most pernicious of all the various forms of opium smoking.

Inspired probably more by hatred of the foreigners who became enriched by the importation of the drug than by any feeling of humanity, the Chinese authorities continued for two whole centuries to inflict all manner of punishments on those who smoked opium, no matter in what form. The offenders were fined, thrown into prison, compelled to wear the cangue, or heavy wooden collar, fitting closely round the neck and preventing the victim from obtaining any rest, or received a varying number of strokes from the bamboo on the mouth or on the soles of the feet. Now, however, all is changed, for the tax imposed on opium brings wealth to the coffers of the Government, and although smoking is still nominally forbidden, it is in reality encouraged throughout the length and breadth of the land.

Opinion is very much divided as to the effect of opium on those who indulge in it. When I was in Indo-China I was only able to consult English doctors on the subject, and it was impossible not to feel that they were necessarily prejudiced in favour of the drug, bearing in mind the great revenues reaped by their Government from its importation. I was assured by one of them that its use in moderation was perfectly harmless, and that an old confirmed smoker if suddenly deprived of it, does not suffer any ill effects. This, by the way, is a very important point. My informants cited cases of ardent consumers of opium being thrown into prison, where such a thing as a pipe was not to be had; yet instead of suffering from the deprivation, the victims retained their usual health, and were not nearly so much affected as sailors would be who could not have the tobacco to which they are accustomed, or drunkards cut off from every beverage but pure water. It will be remembered that after the suppression of the Commune in France in 1871, many of the insurgents sent to Brest died at once from the sudden loss of the stimulants they had become accustomed to. More hardened or more philosophical, who shall say which? the Chinese prisoners deprived of their best-beloved pastime resign themselves without a murmur, though there is no doubt that they suffer frightfully from the terrible conditions in the gaols, coming out, if they come out alive, mere skeletons. A "Celestial" place of detention is indeed a Gehenna of horror and misery. It is only fair to add, however, that a case occurred of a man, who before he was sent to prison had never missed his pipe for thirty years, yet he gained three pounds in weight during the first three weeks of his detention.

Amongst the poorer classes in China it is really the time and money wasted on the drug which are of more importance to the bread-winner than the bad effect on his health. At the best of times the wages earned by a Chinese labourer are extremely low, and when he takes to smoking, his wife and children suffer much, as do those of drunkards in Europe. Archibald Little, who knows the Celestials as well perhaps as any other Englishman, says that during his "forty years' stay in the country and extensive intercourse with every class, he has met with few natives seriously injured by the drug. To the well-nourished Chinaman," he adds, "his evening pipes are more a pastime, a means of passing the time pleasantly in a state of placid inactivity dear to the Oriental, while the merchant conducts many of his best bargains over the pipe, much as negotiations are often conducted over a bottle of wine at home. . . . It is when," adds this keen observer, "a Chinese mandarin succumbs to the opium-pipe and spends most of his time on the opium-couch that the mischief is serious, for rapacity and mis-government go on unchecked,"[1] it being all but impossible to get such a man removed from his post. He has, say the natives, the 'Yin,' their name for the passionate craving for the drug, corresponding with what is called dipsomania by European doctors, and there is no hope for him; he will indulge his passion till he dies. Not unjustly have many medical men called

[1] *Through the Yang-tse Gorges*, p. 194.

FIG. 42.—AN OPIUM-SMOKER.

attention to the indulgence in wine and brandy of the European residents in China, especially in Hong-Kong, and suggested that the missionaries should begin their reforms at home, and before inveighing against Chinese vices they should endeavour to win converts to sobriety amongst their own fellow-countrymen.

In discussing the evil effects of opium-smoking, the very great value of the drug as a medicine is liable to be forgotten, yet the lives of thousands have been saved by its use under proper control. It has absolutely no rival in its power of giving needful sleep in illness and in relieving pain, whilst in many diseases its effect is of the greatest possible advantage to the patient.

Dr. Ayres of Hong-Kong relates several experiments he made in his own person to test the truth of the theory that the poisonous qualities of opium evaporate when it is smoked, but remain active when it is eaten. He began by absorbing a very small quantity per day till he could take as much as half-an-ounce, and says that he experienced sensations so intensely agreeable that he realized what the suffering of deprivation must be when the habit of opium-eating is once confirmed. He then tried smoking a pipe of the prepared drug every day, without feeling any ill effects whatever; there was, he declares, absolutely no difference in his pulse or in his temperature. It was exactly the same with several Europeans whom he persuaded to follow his example. "I counted the throbs of their pulse, I took their temperature, and there was absolutely nothing abnormal about either, although I had made them smoke twelve pipes each." This does but prove that the effects of opium are different with different constitutions,

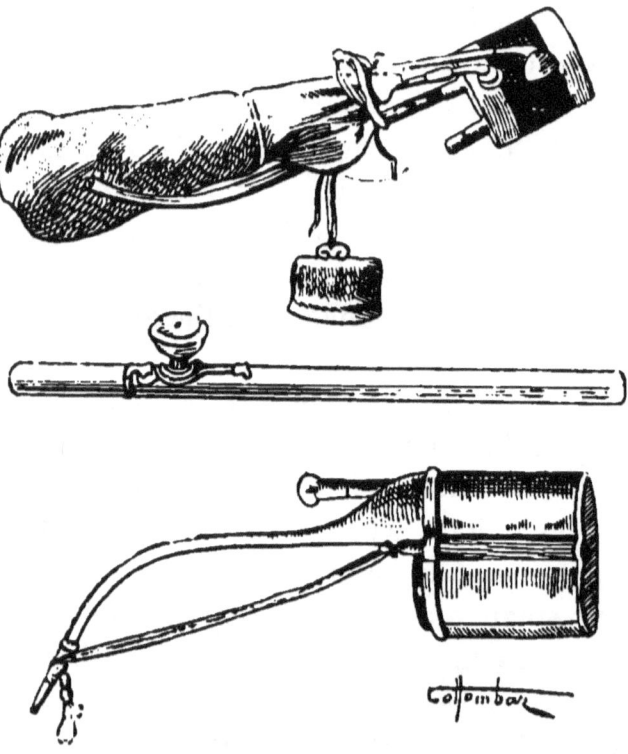

FIG. 43.—OPIUM PIPES.

and that there are some who can take it even in large quantities with impunity; but for all that the horrors of the so-called black smoke, and of the opium dens of China can hardly be exaggerated, even the Celestials themselves admitting that the effects of the drug are injurious to health, and warp the better nature of those who indulge in it to excess; but, as already remarked, its price is still so high that only the wealthy can afford it in quantities likely to be hurtful. It is as difficult for a Chinese workman to get opium as it would be for a French peasant to buy champagne, or an English apprentice to indulge in port-wine. Moreover, it is even now the exception for rich Celestials to yield themselves body and soul to the temptation. One opium-smoker goes to call on another, and the two indulge in a friendly pipe together as they chat about the weather, or the state of trade, or perhaps arrange a marriage for a son or a daughter; but the host does not expect to see his guest fall asleep and roll on the ground like a pig, any more than a European now-a-days expects his visitor to succumb to drink, and slip under the table as was so common an occurrence at the beginning of the nineteenth century. The ordinary opium-smoker does not light his pipe to induce sleep, but just to enable him to forget his troubles for a time, and no De Quincey or Sylvestre de Sacy is needed to prove that a man in rags may indulge in happy dreams of prosperity without leaving some cheap and dingy tavern. Still we cannot fail to contrast the ugly Chinese apparatus with all its paraphernalia, including the horribly smelling lamp needed to keep it alight, with the simple European pipe, so easily filled to begin with, and so readily replenished. The lover of opium seeks to be alone; he has no desire for the

SOCIABLE SMOKERS 183

company of even his dearest friend in his den; but the smoker of the comparatively innocent weed delights in gathering his comrades about him, and there is nothing in the wide world more provocative of good fellowship than the fumes of tobacco.

FIG. 44.—REQUISITES FOR OPIUM-SMOKING.

CHAPTER X

Missionary effort in China—First arrival of the Jesuits—Landing of Michael Roger—Adam Schaal appointed Chief Minister of State—The scientific work of the Jesuits—Affection of the young Emperor Kang-Hi for them—Arrival of other monks—Disputes between them and the Jesuits—The Pope interferes—Fatal results for the Christians—Speech of Kang-Hi—Expulsion of the Jesuits—Concessions to Europeans in newly opened ports—Hatred of foreigners at Tien-tsin—Arrival of French nuns—Their mistakes in ignoring native feeling—Chinese children bought by the Abbé Chevrier—A Chinese merchant's views on the situation—Terrible accusations against the Sisters—Murder of the French Consul and his assistant—The Governor of Tien-tsin responsible—Massacre of the Abbé Chevrier and one hundred children—The Lady Superior and her nuns cut to pieces and burnt—The guilty Governor Chung-Ho sent to Paris as envoy—No proper vengeance exacted by the French—Other Sisters go to Tien-tsin.

THERE is no more pathetic, no more thrilling story in all the annals of Christianity than that of missionary effort in China, and those who remember the sad fate of the French Sisters at Tien-tsin, and of many other devoted women, will not fail to accord their tribute of admiration to the noble devotion which has inspired so many to lay down their lives in the sacred cause of the propagation of the Gospel in the Celestial Empire. That the crop of proselytes yielded by a soil fructified with the blood of virgin martyrs is altogether out of proportion to the expenditure of life and money involved in winning them, is indeed a melancholy fact ; but undaunted by the terrors of the past, fresh bands of eager zealots are ever ready to take the place of those worsted in the struggle, and at the present moment there seems hope that the religion of the Redeemer may yet take real root in the districts newly opened to European trade.

As is well known, it was the Jesuits who were the first to succeed in introducing Christianity into China. Far more enlightened and worldly-wise than the monks of the rival orders, they obtained a footing where so many others had failed, by their tact in giving out that they were pilgrims from the West who had heard of the wonders of the Celestial Empire, and had come to it to see those wonders with their own eyes.

The pioneer of these astute followers of Ignatius Loyola was a certain Michael Roger, who landed in China in 1581, and although some of his successors were beheaded in 1615 the work they had done bore fruit in the erection of a church at Kei-Fung-Fu, on the Yellow River, in which quite a number of converts attended the Roman Catholic services. This church was destroyed through the bursting of a dyke, and the Jesuit missionary then in charge of it was drowned in trying to save his little flock. In spite of this catastrophe, however, the Jesuits continued to gain ground, and during the reign of the Emperor Shun-Che, who occupied the throne from 1644 to 1662, China was actually for some little time governed by Adam Schaal, a member of that community, who had been made Chief Minister of State on account of his wisdom. Another Jesuit, Father Ferdinand Verbiest, held a high astronomical appointment, for then as now the heavenly bodies were studied with intense eagerness in the Celestial Empire, and many officers of State were specially told off to report on everything connected with them.

The successor of Shun-Che, his son Kang-Hi, who was only eight years old when he came to the throne, showed special aptitude for astronomy, and was never tired of listening to the instructions of Father Verbiest. As he grew older he worked with him and the other missionaries at geometry and the kindred sciences, gaining year by year in scientific knowledge. It was during his reign that the Jesuit missionaries, Bouvet, Regis, Fartoux, Fridelli, Cardoso, and others, made their celebrated survey of the whole of China on trigometrical principles, which is still looked upon as absolutely correct by geographers, and there is little doubt that had the gifted young Emperor been left entirely under the guidance of these enlightened fathers, they would, through the door opened by science, have introduced Christianity, or rather their form of Christianity, throughout the entire Empire. During the minority of Kang-Hi, however, the four ministers appointed to govern the country did all in their power to counteract the influence of the foreigners, and restore all the old-established customs. Their efforts were aided by the fact that monks belonging to other orders had now established themselves here and there in the country, and between them and the Jesuits a bitter feud was waged as to the way in which Christian worship should be performed, and the meaning of certain Chinese words. To give but one or two instances of the puerile nature of the quarrel which jeopardized the cause that should have been sacred to all the disputants, one side claimed that the word *Chang-ti* signified the material heaven, the other that it referred to the God inhabiting heaven; one side considered the honour shown to ancestors and the reverence in which the doctrines of Confucius are held to be religious duties, whilst the other looked upon them as mere civil or political customs. That it was of little consequence which was right was patent to any but the most prejudiced observer, yet the foolish monks referred their differences for arbitration to the Pope and the Emperor. The former decided in favour of the Dominicans, the latter in that of the Jesuits, and the Chinese literati not unreasonably asked how the missionaries could expect to be listened to by the natives if they could not agree amongst themselves.

All might, however, even yet have been well, and the Jesuits might have continued their education of the young Emperor had not the Pope unfortunately sent a legate to Pekin charged with the difficult task of making the Jesuits conform to the views of their opponents. This roused the wrath and jealousy of the Emperor, who, of course, knew nothing about the Pope, and did more to undermine the power of his hitherto trusted advisers than anything else could have done. He had, he said, allowed Christianity to be preached just as he had had other religions, but only on condition that the moral precepts inculcated by the first philosopher of the country, and accepted by all the most enlightened amongst his people, were left unquestioned, yet here was an envoy sent from some unknown land with instructions to tamper with the belief of his subjects. An Imperial edict was therefore issued in 1706, ordering the expulsion of all missionaries without distinction of sect; the Christian churches were desecrated and destroyed, and all natives who had embraced the new doctrine were persecuted with the utmost severity, fined, imprisoned, and in some cases put to death. Then the Pope from his distant throne in Rome sent yet another legate, bearing a letter protesting in the strongest terms against these severe measures, but Kang-Hi, who certainly had considerable reason on his side, called his notables together, and having informed them of the contents of the Holy Father's missive exclaimed: "This epistle ignores every one but these vile Europeans, yet how can they decide anything about the great doctrine of the Chinese, whose very language these people from Europe do not understand? From the way these Christians behave, it strikes me that there is some resemblance between the practices of their sect and those of certain impious bonzes of our own land. We must now forbid Europeans from preaching their faith amongst us if we wish to prevent the recurrence of disagreeable events." The division of the sexes until after marriage was then, as now, one of the most rigidly-observed customs of the Celestials, and it is probable that the "evil practices" referred to in the speech quoted above, were the meeting of men and women for worship in the same building. This was more shocking to Chinese public opinion than anything else, and may have had something to do with this final failure of missionary effort. Kang-Hi was, there is no doubt, a very enlightened ruler, and, moreover, himself a writer of considerable talent. He compiled a dictionary of the Chinese and Manchu dialects, translated the five sacred books of China into the Tartar language, and wrote many interesting essays on various subjects. Moreover it was thanks to his initiative, that a very complete Chinese dictionary was produced by thirty of the chief literati of his time.

Kang-Hi, who, in spite of the fulmination of the

great edict against the Christians, still in his heart cherished a strong affection for the Jesuits, who had won his love through the interest they had taken in his favourite pursuits, was succeeded by his son, Young-t-Ching who inherited none of his father's sympathy for Europeans, and persecuted the Christians with the utmost severity. His advisers represented to him, " that the missionaries had deceived the late Emperor, and that that monarch had lost a great deal of *prestige* by his encouragement of the Jesuits." Moreover, the viceroys of outlying provinces sent accounts of the iniquities of the converts to the new faith in their districts, the governor of Fu-Kian distinguishing himself especially by the bitterness of his rancour against them. He begged the Emperor in the interests of his people to banish all foreigners without distinction to Macao, then already occupied by the Portuguese.

It was, however, fortunately for the Chinese as well as for the foreigners, one thing to issue these sweeping denunciations, and another to have them fully carried out. Europeans were too useful at the Court of Pekin for the Emperor to be willing to part with them all, and he naïvely decided to keep those about him who were of any service to him, but to banish the rest. The missionaries of the capital who were thus reprieved, hoped to win help for their colleagues of the provinces by writing to a brother of the Emperor, who they believed to be favourable to them, and they received the following disinterested reply: "We have no intention of imitating your way of going on in Europe; your disputes about our customs have done you a great deal of harm, and China will miss nothing when you are no longer there." Moreover the Emperor added a postscript to this letter, which ran thus: "What would you say if I sent a troop of Buddhist priests into your country? When your Father Ricci was here there were only a few of you; you had not then disciples and churches in all the provinces. It was only during the reign of my father that you increased with such rapidity; we saw it then, but we did not dare say anything about it. If, however, you deceived my father, do not hope that you will deceive me too. . . . You want all the Chinese to become Christians; your religion requires it, I know, but what would become of us then? In times of trouble the people would listen to no voice but yours." This naïve and unanimous testimony to the potency of the Christian faith must have been rather cheering than depressing to those to whom it was addressed, and that they did not fail to perceive that their Imperial enemy was no ordinary man is proved by the eulogy pronounced on him by Father Du Halde, who says: "It is impossible to help admiring his indefatigable application to work; day and night his thoughts are occupied on the establishment of a wise government which will secure the well-being of his subjects; to please him, you have but to propose some project of public utility. . . . He has made several very good regulations with a view to doing honour to merit, and recompensing virtue, for promoting emulation amongst the labouring classes, and to help the people in barren years. These qualities have won for him in a very short time the respect and love of all his subjects."

These quotations throw a luminous side-light upon the character of the Emperor, and make it the more evident how short-sighted was the conduct which led to the breach between his father and the Jesuits. Had the latter continued the policy with which their predecessors had begun, conciliating public opinion by the study of the arts and sciences to which Government and people were alike devoted, instead of splitting straws about doctrine and phraseology, the sad stories of the massacres of defenceless women and children would never have had to be written. It was one of the Jesuit Fathers who gave Kang-Hi his first clock, and another who won the hearts of all the ladies of the court by making a camera-obscura, which enabled them to see something of the outside world from which they were so rigorously excluded. With the expulsion of the Jesuits in the eighteenth century all the work done by them was destroyed, and the missionaries who succeeded them had to contend with the prejudices their short-sighted policy had aroused, as well as with the difficulties inseparable from every attempt to introduce a new religion.

In every port thrown open of recent years to

European commerce the Imperial Government sets aside what are called concessions to the foreign residents, whom the authorities still look upon as unwelcome intruders, though the citizens are not slow to appreciate the difference between their own unsavoury and crowded quarters, and the well-built, airy streets occupied by the English, the French, or the Germans. In these concessions missionaries of pretty well every sect have, of course, hastened to obtain a footing, and volumes might be filled with the record of their struggles, their difficulties, their triumphs, and their defeats. It will be enough for our present purpose to tell of the massacre, referred to above, of the French Sisters at Tien-tsin, for it was alike one of the most horrible and most typical of modern times. By the treaty signed there in 1858 the port was thrown open to foreign trade, and in 1861 a British consulate was established in it. The memory of the sack of Pekin by the Anglo-French forces was still fresh, and the hatred of the foreign devils was fiercer and if possible more bitter in Tien-tsin than elsewhere, for so far its people had had very little intercourse with Europeans. Only amongst the more enlightened of the Chinese was the fact recognized that the time for opposition to the entry of foreigners was gone by, and that if the country were not opened from within, it would be forced from without, and the dismemberment of the Empire become inevitable.

Situated on the right bank of the Pei-ho, Tien-tsin is the port of the capital, from which it is eighty miles distant. It is therefore one of the keys of China, and even before the opening of the railway from it to Pekin in 1897, it was of immense strategic importance. All this of course intensified the jealousy of the Chinese, when the lock was forced, so to speak, by the white skins, and great indeed was the courage needed to face the turbulent population, and endeavour to win proselytes from amongst them. Even in Shanghai, comparatively inured to the presence of the foreign element, nuns had been insulted; a native spitting in the faces of two holy women in the streets, who had done absolutely nothing to provoke hostility.

Yet there were found devoted women who came to reside in Tien-tsin, carrying their lives in their hands, knowing full well what they had to expect, yet determined to face unflinchingly not only the hostility of the natives, but also the rigours of the inhospitable climate, for the river is blocked with ice from December to May, and before the opening of the railway there could be no hope of help from without in the winter, no matter what the emergency.

The Sisters, however, set to work directly they arrived, aided by the French Abbé Chevrier, M. Fontanier, the French Consul, and his assistant, M. Simon. They quickly organized their plan of campaign; some opening a hospital where all sufferers were received, no matter of what nationality or religion, whilst others devoted themselves to the education of the little girls bought by the

THE PURCHASE OF GIRLS

Abbé with the fund known in France as that of the *Sainte-Enfance*, or Holy Infancy. In the school kept by the devoted ladies, the Chinese maidens were lodged, fed, and taught to do different kinds of needlework, as well as educated in the Roman Catholic religion. It was the purchase of the

FIG. 45. A TEMPLE AT TIEN-TSIN.

pupils that was really at the root of the terrible troubles which overtook the Mission. The Celestials, as has already been explained above, are in the habit of buying girls, but for a very different purpose to that of the devoted priests and Sisters. They too have hospitals for the indigent and infirm, but they could not be brought to believe that the missionaries received the children merely to feed, educate, and make Christians of them. The rumour quickly spread, not only in Tien-tsin, but in Shanghai and elsewhere, that good money was to be got by selling children to the Sisters, and certain natives at once set to work to kidnap little ones with a view to securing what they thought would be a lucrative trade. So many girls were stolen, and the missionaries lent so much colour to the accusation against them of connivance by the increasing number of their *protégées* that public feeling was thoroughly aroused. The cry of "Stealers of children" was raised, and foreigners, especially the French, had stones thrown at them in the streets.

There is no doubt that if the missionaries had been wise, they would have given up receiving children for a time, whether in the orphanage or the hospital, but religious zeal was not in this case tempered with discretion, and terrible indeed were the results of this short-sighted policy. Of course all the girls rescued by the nuns were not bought, but a great many of them were, for the Chinese law encourages the selling of female children. Moreover, if calumnies were circulated about foreigners, they in their turn did not hesitate to spread reports of the unnatural way in which Chinese mothers treated their children, and much was written on the subject in the reports sent home. I, however, can testify from personal inquiry that these were quite unfounded libels. In Canton every one I questioned on the subject repudiated the accusations with the greatest indignation. There was, however, the question to which I never could get a satisfactory reply, and that was, " Is it true that the Chinese cause the death of deformed children at their birth ? " Evasive answers were always made to this downright inquiry, but with regard to healthy, well-formed infants of either sex, I will quote verbatim what a wealthy Chinese merchant of very influential position said to me :

"It is unfortunately true," he said, "that children have sometimes been abandoned by Chinese mothers, but only under very sad circumstances, generally the failure of the harvest. Do you know what has led to some of your priests accusing the Chinese of being unnatural parents, mere brutes resembling cats and dogs ? It is because now and then our teeming population of four hundred million souls is visited by terrible and extraordinary misfortunes, such as a sudden outbreak of the cholera or the plague, which are, however, among the least of our troubles, for even more frequent, more destructive to life, is the famine which occurs every year, now in the north, now in the south, now in the east, now in the west. If the rice-crop fail through a dry season, thirty or fifty millions of human creatures are in danger of perishing from hunger if sufficient relief does not reach them in time. We have not the means you in Europe have of speedy communication between our provinces; we have no railways, no fleets of steamers to take grain from one place to another.

Well, what happens? Just what occurs when some town or island is blockaded in war. Old men and children perish first, and if a few of the infants do survive, what can the mothers do but thrust them away from them when the milk in their breasts is all dried up? Under these circumstances you may see able-bodied men eating such things as rats, snakes, and vermin, which the Chinese are accused of devouring with delight even in times of plenty. I know nothing about the history of your country, but you ought to know it well. Will you swear to me that there has never been a time when women have been driven to let their children die for want of nourishment and warmth? You do not answer. So it is evident that terrible things such as this have happened in Europe. Well now, would it not be downright unfair of me, if knowing this to be truth, I turned your silence against you by preaching throughout China that French mothers, like those in China, fling their children into the gutter?"

Was not this a sensible speech?—and would it not be well if missionaries were equally wise in their way of looking at things? Is it not a pity that so many enthusiastic young men and women should be sent to meet a terrible death in a vain effort to alter what cannot be changed? Those who sanction the going forth of these bands of devoted martyrs do not make sufficient allowance for the fact that the indifference of the Chinese to Christianity is really a part of their own religion

They cultivate stoicism, they never allow anything to upset their *sangfroid*, but meet torture and death with equal composure. It is a hopeless task to endeavour to rouse them to enthusiasm about anything. It would be wiser to leave their conversion alone. All this does not, however, detract in any way from the heroism of the Sisters at Tien-tsin, who, in spite of the ever-increasing hostility to them, went on doing their charitable work, unheeding the danger in which they must have known they stood.

It was on June 22, 1870, that fatal year for France, just before the breaking out of the Franco-German War, when the relations between the French Government and that of Pekin were considerably strained, that the long-smouldering fire broke into flame in Tien-tsin. The Governor, Chung-Ho by name, a Tartar by birth, a kindly man enough, but far too weak for the position he held, was really responsible for the massacre, though he endeavoured to shelter himself from responsibility behind the mandarins, whom he ought to have controlled. The rising against the foreigners had evidently been preconcerted, for there was really no apparent cause for the sudden rush of the bravos upon their victims. It has been said that the French Consul, M. Fontanier, who was the first to fall beneath the blows of the assassins, really gave the signal for the massacre by presenting his revolver at the head of the Governor, but this of course was only an excuse, and nothing could really have averted the catastrophe.

From nine in the morning to five in the afternoon of the terrible day the killing went on, the French being hunted through the streets and struck down, often on the very thresholds of their houses. After the murder of the French consul, his interpreter, M. Thomassin, and his young wife were attacked; and in a futile attempt to save the latter Thomassin was terribly wounded. He managed to fling himself into the canal, which flows near the Consulate, but the literati were determined that he should not escape, and he was dispatched in the water. Meanwhile, as a shepherd calls his flock together when the wolves are threatening, the Abbé Chevrier had collected around him the orphan children to the number of one hundred then under the care of the missionaries; but they were all massacred, the good priest dying amongst them. A French merchant and his wife, with three Russians who were mistaken for Frenchmen, were also murdered.

The Sisters in the orphanage and hospital were, strange to say, the last to hear of the awful scenes being enacted in the streets. Secure in their belief that they had done no evil, and that, therefore, no one could wish to harm them, they quietly went on with their work, and did not even demand the protection of the Chinese authorities. This would, however, probably have been powerless to save them; for it was the mandarins who had been most active in circulating slanders against them, saying that they used the eyes of children for making some of their medicines, and spreading all manner of other silly reports. The simple-minded Sisters had only laughed when told of these slanders, but they would have been wiser to try and refute them, for they were believed by the common people as readily as stories about witches were in Europe not so very long ago.

The sun was already setting, lighting up the streets reddened with the blood of the innocent, when the murderers, their rage increased by the ease with which they had killed their victims, seem suddenly to have remembered that there were defenceless women at the orphanage still to be destroyed, and with one accord they rushed to the doors clamouring for admittance. Their shouts being unheeded, they lost no time in breaking down the door, and found the Superior of the Sisterhood calmly waiting to receive them. Alas! her fortitude availed her nothing; she was brutally seized, dragged to a post not far off and bound to it. Then ensued a scene too horrible for description; the fiends in human shape danced round their helpless victim, and inflicted on her all the tortures in which the Chinese are so terribly skilled, finally cutting her body into small pieces. The terrified nuns kneeling on the steps of their little chapel in agonized prayer were one and all first outraged and then murdered, their home and church were set fire to, and their mangled bodies flung into the flames. One poor young girl had had the sense to disguise herself as a Chinese, and was hastening towards the English Consulate to take refuge there, when unfortunately she was recognized and murdered by some Chinese soldiers.

Not one French man or woman escaped, and the indignation throughout France when the terrible news arrived can be imagined.

As usual, the Imperial Government was profuse in apologies and excuses, for well did the Emperor and his advisers know how terrible might be the vengeance exacted by France for the blood of her children. A few Chinese heads were cut off —in China heads are of little account,—and it was determined at Pekin that a very high official should be sent to Paris to make due apology, and promise that nothing of the kind should occur again. It was of course difficult to decide who should be entrusted with this delicate mission, and the choice actually fell on Chung-Ho, the Governor of Tien-tsin, the very man, as has been seen, to whose culpable neglect the tragedy was due. But for the fact that the unfortunate country of France was then in the throes of her most awful experience of modern times, the probability is that the blood-stained Tartar would have met with a reception in its capital very little to his taste. As things were, however, no one in France suspected who he really was, public attention was concentrated on the war. The death of the French missionaries in remote Tien-tsin was already forgotten in the anguish of defeat, and the necessity for organizing the defence against the ruthless invaders. The Empire had fallen; the Emperor was a prisoner in the hands of the Germans—safer there than he would have been amongst his own disillusioned subjects. The interview with M. Thiers was put off again and again, until at last a comparatively leisure time was secured. Then, alas! that I should have to write it, the Chinese traitor was presented to the Chief of the State with all the ceremonial due to foreign ambassadors. He was escorted to the Elysée in a state-carriage by a guard of cuirassiers, and received with all the usual honours.

No good result ensued for French interests in China from this interview, and soon after the return of the envoy to his native country, yet another missionary, M. Hué, was assassinated in the province of Se-Tchuen; whilst not far from the scene of the murder of Margary, related in a previous chapter, two priests were burnt alive, and four of their proselytes cut to pieces.

But enough of these horrors, I must dwell on them no more, for I have no wish to intensify race hatred, or to raise French feeling against a nation with which we have a treaty of peace. I must, however, add just one word to show how indomitable is the missionary spirit in the religious orders of France. In 1876, when the country was beginning to settle down after the awful events of the preceding years, that is to say, six years after the massacre at Tien-tsin, another party of Sisters went to that very town to begin again the work of charity so tragically interrupted, although it was well known that there was no abatement in the bitterness of the feeling against foreigners, and that the mandarins were especially averse to female missionaries. The unselfish devotion, seeking for no earthly reward, of the saintly nuns is well illustrated by the reply made to me when I went to the head-quarters of the Sisterhood in the *Rue de Bac*, Paris, and asked the Lady Superior to give me the names of the martyrs of 1870 that I might render to them the honour so justly due. Those names were refused, " for," said the austere head of the order, " our nuns have won the greatest of all rewards already, and that is enough."

The new-comers to the site watered by the blood of the innocent, have proceeded exactly on the same lines as their predecessors ; they opened a hospital and some schools, apparently in total ignorance of the dangers surrounding them. A tri-colour flag floats once more from the buildings under their control. The " Cyclamens," as lovers of flowers call the caps worn by the devoted Sisters, are once more familiar objects in the streets of Tien-tsin. May their labour of love be rewarded as it deserves, and may God temper the wind to them as He does to the lambs shorn of their fleece, for truly they sorely need the protection of Heaven in their defenceless condition! Fortunately, however, they are no longer so isolated as were the pioneers of missionary effort in 1870. In 1881 the port of Tien-tsin became connected by telegraph with Shanghai, where there is a large foreign population, and the Chinese have of late years had so many proofs that foreigners are not to be massacred or in any way injured with impunity, that there is some hope of the avoidance for the future of such tragedies as that we have recorded here.

CHAPTER XI

The Great Wall—Its failure as a defence—Forced labour—Mode of construction—Shih-Hwang-Ti orders all books to be burnt—Mandarins flung into the flames—The *Shu-King* is saved—How the sacred books came to be written—The sedan-chair and its uses—Modern hotels at Pekin—Examination of students for degrees—Cells in which they are confined—Kublai Khan conquers China—Makes Pekin his capital—Introduces paper currency—The Great Canal—Address to the three Philosophers—Marco Polo's visit to Pekin—His description of the Emperor—Kublai Khan's wife—Foundation of the Academy of Pekin—Hin-Heng and his acquirements—Death of Kublai Khan—Inferiority of his successors—Shun-Ti the last Mongol Emperor—Pekin in the time of the Mongols—When seen by Lord Macartney—The city as it is now.

IT is a relief to turn from the terrible events which have given to Tien-tsin such a sinister notoriety to visit from it the celebrated Great Wall of China, the western termination of which is at no great distance from the town on the north. Begun by the Emperor Shih-Hwang-Ti, in B.C. 214, as a protection against the invasions of the Tartars, it was completed in the marvellously short time of five years, that energetic monarch sparing neither expense nor trouble, and ruthlessly sacrificing the lives of thousands of his subjects in his determination to keep out the hated barbarians. That he was not successful, but that his rampart in due time served his enemies better than it had done himself, is one of those ironies of fate with which the student of history is familiar. Tartars, Mongols,

FIG. 46.—THE GREAT WALL.
(*Univers Pittoresque.*)

and Manchus have in their turn reigned over China from the sacred city, within the very defences supposed to be impregnable; the mighty wall remaining a standing proof, not of the wisdom, but of the short-sightedness of its builder.

To secure a sufficient number of men to work at his wall, Shih-Hwang-Ti issued an edict ordering every third labourer throughout the whole of the Empire to labour at it, and the unfortunate men thus selected were forced to work like slaves, with no wages but a scanty supply of food, their places when they fell down dead being quickly taken by other victims. The wall, when completed at the cost of so great an expenditure of human life, was fifteen hundred miles long; its breadth at the bottom was nearly twenty-five feet, and at the top fifteen feet, whilst it varied in height from fifteen to thirty feet. The materials employed would, it is said, be enough to build a wall six feet high and two feet thick to go twice round the world. Six horsemen could ride abreast upon it, and it was fortified by very strong towers, placed at regular intervals of about one hundred yards, that is to say, within two arrow-shots of each other, so that any one attempting to scale it would be covered from one tower or another by the guards stationed in them. The construction of the wall was very strong, the outside being formed of stone and brickwork, whilst the inside was filled up with earth. The wall started from the sea-shore at the Shan-Hai Pass, in N. Lat. 40° and E. Long. 119° 50′, and ran over mountains, through valleys, and across rivers by means of arches, which are still marvels of engineering skill, to the most western province of Kan-su, where it ends at the Khiya Pass. Whilst only insignificant relics now remain of the immense Roman walls which once intersected England and France, this vast monument of an ambitious ruler still stands, ranking as one of the wonders of the world, an incidental proof that at the time of its erection, two thousand years ago, China must have already been a great and civilized Empire. There is no doubt that Shih-Hwang-Ti did succeed in centralizing authority, and absorbing the power of the numerous military chiefs who before his time reigned in the various small kingdoms, making up what is now the Celestial Empire. Unfortunately, however, the monarch aimed rather at his own aggrandizement than at the good of his people, and his vainglorious desire to be looked upon as the founder of the Chinese monarchy led him to issue that celebrated edict, ordering all books and writings referring to his predecessors to be burnt, which inflicted an incalculable loss on future students of history. Those who endeavoured to evade this sweeping decree were to be punished by death, and according to some accounts, hundreds of literati were burnt on piles of the MSS. they had tried to save. In spite of all precautions, however, some few copies of the works of Confucius and other great writers were successfully hidden and brought out again on the death of the tyrant.

On this interesting subject Father Gaubil, in his valuable work on Chinese Chronology, says: " One thing is certain . . . the books containing the geographical surveys and the departmental records were not burnt . . . though the minister Lis-sse, like the Emperor himself, wished the people to remain ignorant, and know nothing about how the country was governed by the earlier kings, or to hear of the great and virtuous men of the past, or

BURNING OF MSS. 209

of the precepts left behind by them." It was this same minister, the Father tells us, who introduced the salutary reform of the use of one character only

FIG. 47.—BURNING OF MANDARINS AND HISTORICAL DOCUMENTS, BY ORDER OF SHIH-KWANG-TI. (*Univers Pittoresque.*)

throughout the Empire, whereas before his time several different kinds of letters were employed in writing. This alphabet was known as the *li-chu*, and is supposed to be identical with that of the present day.

It was indeed fortunate that so many important manuscripts were saved from the general holocaust the sacrilegious Emperor had ordered, for had the *Shu-King* been destroyed, it would have been difficult to give any real account of the China of the past. This most celebrated and authentic of ancient books is supposed to have been begun about the year 2266 B.C., in the reign of the great Yao, brother of that King Ti-Ko, who introduced the polygamy still practised in China. This book, or rather collection of books, is to the Celestials what the Bible is to the Jews, the Koran to the Mahomedans, the Law-Book of Manu to the Hindus, and the Gospel to Christians. It is the very fountain-head of Chinese law, and not to be acquainted with its contents is to be unworthy of holding any place of trust in the Empire. Its authenticity is absolutely established, for it is well known that ever since the year 2637 B.C. there has been a historic Tribunal in Pekin, whose members are chosen from amongst the most distinguished literati of the whole Empire. Once appointed, these scholars can never be removed from office, and it is their duty to register daily everything of importance that occurs in any town, including meteorological and other natural phenomena, as well as what may be called purely historical events, such as the revolts, sieges, fires, and other misfortunes to which humanity is subject.

THE *SHU-KING*

Father Amiot, a very cultivated and intelligent French missionary, says on the subject of the sacred books of the *Shu-King:* "The Chinese annals are superior to the historical documents of every other nation, because there is less fabulous matter in them, and because they are more ancient . . . and more full of information of every kind . . . They are worthy of our fullest confidence, because the epochs to which they refer are determined by astronomical observations, and the accounts of the events of all kinds which occur in those epochs can be mutually checked, and are found, when compared, to prove the good faith of the writers who have transmitted them to us."

They are indeed simply invaluable to the student, forming as they do absolutely trustworthy guides to their researches into the early history of China, carrying it back for long centuries, or rather sexagenaries, for, as already remarked, the Chinese chronology reckons by sixties, not hundreds of years. One incidental proof of their veracity is the fact that their writers, when not fully informed, have left gaps in their narratives instead of filling them up as so many chroniclers would have done with imaginary matter.

They are moreover works of literature rather than mere dry historical documents, and there is no series of books in the whole world on which so many able men have been employed as on the sacred records of the Chinese nation.

What tales the literati might have told in those

old days of their adventures on their way to the capital to take up their work as chroniclers! Even when I made the journey from Tien-tsin to Pekin, before the opening of the railway, I had variety enough, travelling now by boat, now in a palanquin, now in a sedan-chair, and sometimes on horseback, and things must have been far worse in those early days of the beginning of history. One shudders to think of what our own diplomatic agents must have gone through when, after much difficulty, they did at last obtain the coveted honour of representing the Western powers in the chief city of the Celestial Empire. They must have suffered horribly, the more that their presence was thoroughly unwelcome, and it was the delight of every petty official to throw obstacles in their way. The old literati, on the other hand, were treated with the greatest respect, and except when they happened to make some mistake in their astronomical calculations, when their heads paid the forfeit, they lived in considerable luxury.

Pekin, though still not exactly the place Europeans would choose to live in, is now comparatively civilized, and in the spacious rooms of the European ambassadors the foreign residents dine, sup, and dance very much as they would in the capitals of their own countries. Thanks to the seclusion of the sedan-chairs, even ladies can go about without attracting notice, or having to pick their way through the ill-smelling rubbish which still encumbers the streets. No traveller in China with the slightest self-respect goes on foot, and any foreigner who attempts walking lays himself open to every insult. "A chair," says a writer who knows China well, "is far more effective than a passport," and the ambassadors and ambassadresses, the secretaries of legation, the consuls and their wives, employ large numbers of coolies to carry them to and fro. There is something truly wonderful in the way in which a mere handful of Europeans live their own lives, following their own customs, in the midst of a population of three hundred thousand Tartars, Mongols, and Manchus, not to speak of the four hundred thousand Chinese citizens, and the hundred thousand soldiers forming the garrison.

Pekin now actually boasts of two bakers who make bread of fine American flour, and are largely patronized by the foreign residents; and in the markets, the native cooks who cater for the Embassies, find plenty of variety for the tables of their employers at a very reasonable price, including two kinds of pheasant, the grey and the red-legged partridge. Wild geese and wild duck, the hare, the boar, the antelope and the roebuck are also all plentiful, and mutton can be had as tender as that of Wales, Normandy, or the Ardennes.

Not so very long ago, visitors to Pekin had to go to wretched inns where they were far from welcome, or to ask hospitality from the foreign residents, but now there are two hotels where travellers are as well treated as in the West. One, called the Hôtel Français, is kept by a jovial Chinaman, who was at one time cook to an English diplomatist; the other, called the German Hotel, is managed by a burly native of Frankfort, who reminds me of nothing so much as of a Heidelberg tun. In these two inns the rooms are big, with wide chimneys and good windows, so that really it is possible to be quite comfortable in them, even

FIG. 48.—A STREET IN PEKIN.

in winter, if one can avoid the streets, with their deep mud or dust, as the case may be.

It is to Pekin that thousands of students who have already won the second degree of rank, as literati, flock to compete for the distinction known as the Tsen-Sze, which corresponds to some extent with that of a doctor of law in England. The scholar who comes out first in the examinations is considered for the current year the most learned man in all the eighteen provinces of China, and is privileged to choose a post in the very highest department of the Government.

Out of the nine or ten hundred candidates who are examined by the doctors of the Han-Lin College, three hundred are selected, and again tested in the presence of the Emperor. Then ten of these three hundred are picked out to compete once more for the coveted first grade, to win which is the ambition of every literary man in China, for it is equally open to all, though achieved by but few. The ten who are considered worthy are subjected to a very severe final test by a jury selected by the Emperor himself. Their replies to the examination questions are written out, richly bound, and placed before the so-called Son of Heaven, who reads all the manuscripts, and points out the three he considers the best. The authors of these three are raised to first rank, and are *fêted* throughout the capital for three days, marching round it, accompanied by processions bearing flags, beating drums, etc. Of the rest of the three hundred, some become professors at the Han-Lin College, whilst others receive appointments in various parts of the country.

The hall in which the examinations take place has attached to it a number of very small cells, not more than six feet long by three wide and five high—an incidental proof of the average stature of the Chinese—in one of which each candidate is shut up alone, so that the judges may be quite sure his work is all his own. The aspirant to literary honour is even searched to see that he has no books or papers hidden in his robes. He is then supplied with writing materials, and his replies to the questions put to him are not signed, so there is no fear of partiality on the part of the judges. The only furniture of the examination cell is a plank placed across it about fifteen inches above the ground to serve as a seat, and a little tablet fixed to the wall to be used as a desk. There is sometimes such a run upon the cells that a student has to wait for days before he can secure one. Amongst the cells named after the "Red Dragon," the little room is still shown in which the fourth Emperor of the present dynasty worked at certain of the usual examination papers with a view to shedding lustre on the literary life. He had the courage and perseverance to remain shut up in complete seclusion for nine days; but he evidently found the task he had set himself very arduous, for, since his experiment, students have been allowed to come out of their cells every three days to breathe the outer air and stretch their limbs,

FIG. 49.—NIGHT-WATCHMEN IN PEKIN.

The two most interesting facts connected with the history of Pekin are that it is one of the most ancient cities of the world, occupying the site of the capital of the old province of Yen, which is known to have been in existence 1200 years before the Christian era, and that it was made the seat of government by Kublai Khan, the first Mongol Emperor of China, grandson of the mighty conqueror Genghis Khan. This Kublai Khan, though a conqueror and of foreign race, so won the affections of the Chinese that he was justly called the Father of his people, and during his reign the country enjoyed a prosperity never since equalled. The native rulers who had preceded the Mongols had been mere phantom sovereigns, the puppets of their eunuchs and the women of their harems, altogether oblivious of the great example set them by the early monarchs of China.

The warlike and highly civilized Mongols had long since conquered all the districts north and west of the great wall of China, and for years had cast longing eyes at the fertile regions on the other side of that artificial barrier, and when Kublai Khan came to the throne, a mere child, the last survivor of the Soong line was Emperor of China. In this fact the Mongol ruler saw his opportunity, and is said to have sent the following message to the young prince: "Your family owes its rise to the minority of the last Emperor of the preceding dynasty, it is therefore just that you, a child, the last remnant of the line of Soong, should give place to another family."

Whether this Mongol expression of the time-honoured doctrine that might makes right ever reached the ears of the infant prince or not, the approach of the great Khan warriors so terrified the Court, that the Emperor and the ministers took refuge with him on the vessels in the harbour of Canton. There they were followed by the Tartar war-ships, and the terror they inspired was such that the fugitives all flung themselves into the sea, one of the chief grandees being the first to jump overboard with the young Emperor in his arms. More than one hundred soldiers and sailors are supposed to have perished on this fatal day, either from poison, by drowning, or at the hands of the enemy.

This terrible event took place in A.D. 1280 or 1281, when Kublai Khan became sovereign of the whole of China, and fixed his capital at what is now Pekin, but was then called Khan-balegh, or the capital of the Khan. He surrounded his palace with a wall six leagues in circumference, pierced by twelve gateways; the roofs of his residence were very lofty and spacious, richly decorated with gold and silver, and with paintings representing birds, horses, dragons, and other quaint symbolic animals. The roof of the palace was gilded, and six thousand warriors could take shelter in it at one time.

Kublai Khan, who was as wise in statecraft as in battle, took care not to interfere with the institutions of his new subjects; all the officials who submitted to him were allowed to retain their

THE GREAT CANAL

posts, and the Chinese themselves were exempted from military service. This of course concentrated all the power in the hands of the Mongols, and did more than anything else could have done to consolidate the new dynasty, though the Celestials themselves do not seem to have realized its full significance. The new Emperor was visited at his Court of Khan-balegh, or Cambalu, by Marco Polo, that most venturesome traveller and astute observer, whose account of his sojourn with the great Mongol conqueror gives so vivid a picture of life in China in the thirteenth century. Hospitably received by the Khan, the Venetian dwelt much in his book on the magnificence of his court, and makes the sage and humorous remark: "Kublai, who was the first to invent paper-money made from the inner bark of the mulberry-tree, had discovered the true philosopher's stone, for he could create wealth at his own desire."

A far greater boon than the introduction of paper currency was the making of the great canal, which rivals the celebrated wall in the skill of its construction, and has been of far more lasting value to the people of China than that monument of the energy and presumption of Shih-Hwang-Ti. One hundred and seventy thousand men were employed in this useful enterprise, which was not completed until after the death of its promoter. The wonderful waterway, before it fell into disrepair, extended from the capital to Hang-Chan in the province of Che-kiang, and was more than three hundred miles long. Marco Polo said of it: "He (Kublai Khan) has caused a water communication to be made in the shape of a wide and deep channel dug between stream and stream, between lake and lake, forming as it were a great river on which large vessels can ply."

Various sayings of the wise thinker and practical worker, at the head of the newly conquered country, have come down to us. Amongst these may be quoted as specially significant, the address made by the Emperor to three great philosophers whom he had summoned to his presence to aid him in the difficult task of government, in preventing the exodus of the inhabitants from the towns, and the desertion of the country by the cultivators. "You must help me," he said, "to make your fellow-countrymen listen to reason; they look upon us now as if we were bears or tigers; they are afraid of us when we only wish to do them good. My

FIG. 50.—A CHINESE GENERAL IN HIS WAR-CHARIOT.
(*Univers Pittoresque.*)

one desire is to make them happy under my rule, and they will believe it if you tell them so. You, Yao-Theu," he added, "I make general inspector of the agricultural districts; travel about in them, and manage to get them restored to their former owners and cultivated as before; I give you full authority to bring this about."

"As for you, Hin-Heng and Teo-mo, I place the people under your protection; watch over the health and tranquillity of the artisans and workmen, so that they labour as of yore, and that they look forward to enjoying the fruits of their industry in peace. Moreover, I give you full powers to re-open schools wherever they used to be, or to build new ones if you think it desirable; in a word, do all that you think will promote the good of the public —I approve in advance of everything you may decide on."

Long before the time of Richelieu, Kublai Khan formed an academy, to which flocked scholars and men of letters of every nationality. From India, from Persia, and from beyond the Oxus they came, as well as from the different countries of Europe, attracted by the fame of the learning in the Chinese capital. Marco Polo, who for three years was governor of one of the southern provinces of China, became a member of this academy, and Hin-Heng, one of the philosophers alluded to above, also belonged to it, excelling all his *confrères* in the variety of his acquirements. Speaking of him, Father Amiot says: "There was no science he had not studied, and he succeeded in them all ... he gave his attention to chronology, to history, and to music. He was a geometrician and astronomer, and he was one of the savants who worked at the reform of the Chinese almanac ... he was well versed in the ancient history of his nation, he knew the laws and customs of his native land, and explained them so clearly that Kublai Khan entrusted to him the drawing up of the code for his dynasty. To all this knowledge he added that of the Mongol language, in which he composed several excellent works, not to speak of the translations he made of the best Chinese books ... He also made commentaries on the *Shu-King*, or sacred books."

FIG. 51.—PORCELAIN TOWER AT NANKING.

Very vivid is the light thrown by these quotations on the civilization of the capital of China under the Mongol ruler, and, thanks once more to Marco Polo, we are able to form a very accurate idea of the personal appearance of Kublai Khan. "The great Lord of lords," the celebrated traveller tells us, "is of a good stature, neither little nor big, but of medium height . . . his limbs are well formed . . . his face is white, with cheeks like a rose; his nose is well shaped and prominent." The chronicler further tells us that Kublai Khan had four wives, whom he treated exactly alike, and that his eldest, no matter by which mother, would succeed him when he died. According to other authorities, one wife alone enjoyed the title of Empress, and she had three hundred female slaves to attend upon her.

The founder alike of the Mongol, or, as it is sometimes called, the Yuan dynasty, and of Pekin, lived to the advanced age of eighty-three, and was succeeded by his grandson Timur; but able as that prince was, he was by no means equal to his predecessor. Later members of the Tartar race, who occupied the Chinese throne, did not follow the example of the old Manchu rulers, so that the wonderfully-organized government of Kublai Khan gradually fell to pieces, and at the end of seventy-three years yet another new dynasty supplanted that which had appeared so firmly established. No one can wonder at this who reads the stories told of Shun-Ti, the ninth and last Mongol sovereign, who, called to the supreme power at the early age of thirteen, amused himself by watching the dancing of sixteen young girls, called the sixteen spirits, and wasted time and treasure in endeavouring to pry into the future, with the aid of soothsayers, whilst he neglected every duty he owed to God and to his subjects.

Marco Polo left a glowing description of the Imperial Palace at Kambala, or Pekin, where, he tells us, "twice five miles of fertile ground, with walls and towers, were girdled round," and as late as 1793, when Lord Macartney visited the city, he found that it was still very much what it had been in the thirteenth century. On the change of dynasty, after the expulsion of Shun-Ti, the capital was transferred to Nanking, but in 1421 Pekin was restored to its old dignity, and its walls were still further extended. In the following centuries its fortunes fluctuated greatly, and it was not until 1860, when it was taken by the Anglo-French forces, that it began to assume anything of its present appearance. The central or inner city, known as the Manchu, is divided into three parts: the Purple Forbidden Town containing the imperial residences; the Imperial or August City, with the great temples, where the imperial family worship their ancestors; and the general city, beyond which again is the so-called Chinese town, consisting of a net-work of lanes and alleys, with two wide thoroughfares intersecting each other at right angles.

The foreign legations are all grouped together in the south-eastern corner of the August City, and consist of Chinese palaces transformed into a semblance of European houses. The French Legation is the largest, though perhaps not the most comfortable, and is situated in the centre of a very fine park. After describing the imperial palaces, the temples and pagodas of Pekin, and remarking on the great uniformity of their style of architecture, a modern writer, who knows the city well, says: "The chief ornaments of the streets are the fronts of the shops; large panels of carved wood, sometimes gilded, frame the façades, the carvings representing dragons, phœnixes, etc., the effect being very decorative . . . on the other hand, the private houses, with their lofty walls and numerous entrance courts, do nothing to contribute to the beauty of the street." The modern Chinese are ardent lovers of their homes, and the humblest artisan lives alone, with his family, in the strictest seclusion. "There is nothing," adds this true observer, "to distinguish any one house from another, and it is the same with the theatres and opium dens; uniformity is the guiding principle in everything, and even the priests of the various missions have adopted the Chinese customs and mode of plaiting the hair." The town of Pekin is, in fact, unique in the power it seems to have of making all who reside in it conform to one style. It perfectly represents the country of which it is the capital, with its intense hostility to innovation, holding itself aloof from every other nation, ignoring the very existence of the West for more than twenty-five centuries, and only waking up to its existence to despise it as the home of outer barbarians. But of late years there has been change in the very air even of Pekin; the opening of the railway from it to Tien-tsin, two years ago, was indeed a significant sign of the times, and the next decade will doubtless witness the breaking down of convention even in that stronghold of conservatism, the Purple Forbidden City. Already Tartar carts, Chinese chaises, blue and green sedan-chairs, strings of camels, condemned prisoners wearing the fatal cangue, Buddhist priests chanting litanies, and even eunuchs of the Emperor himself, in their black and yellow uniforms, are jostled by riders on horseback or by carriages, but little different from those in use in Paris and London. The West has introduced the thin edge of the wedge of its civilization into the inner citadel, the time-honoured watchword of "China for the Chinese" has lost its conjuring power, and the attempt of the Empress Dowager to revive it can but end in disaster for her and those she rules in such an arbitrary and old-fashioned style.

CHAPTER XII

Fall of the Mongol dynasty—The son of a labourer chosen Emperor—He founds the Ming dynasty—Choo becomes Tae-tsoo, and rules with great wisdom—He dies and leaves his kingdom to his grandson—Young-lo attacks and takes Nanking—The young Emperor burnt to death—Young-lo is proclaimed Emperor, and makes Pekin his capital—First European visits China—Tartar chief usurps supreme power—Dies soon after—Foundation of present dynasty—Accession of Shun-Che—Chinese compelled to shave their heads—The old style of coiffure in China—Care of the modern pig-tail.

THE fall of the Mongol dynasty and final banishment of the last Emperor of that once famous race was brought about by a young Chinese bonze named Choo, the son of a labourer, who joined the rebels when they rose against the foreign ruler. A delicate boy unfit for out-door toil, he had been placed by his father in a monastery to be educated, but he early became tired of the inactive life, and enlisted in the Imperial army as a common soldier. He soon distinguished himself, and rapidly rose to a position of high rank, when he married a widow with a fortune, belonging to a family disaffected towards the Government. Soon after the wedding an insurrection broke out at Nanking, and thanks to the influence of his bride the young Choo was chosen leader. So great was his popularity that thousands flocked to his standard, and after winning several victories he led an army against Pekin itself. The capital was taken, Shan-Ti and his family driven into exile, and with one accord the people proclaimed their beloved General Choo Emperor. This was in 1366, and the Ming dynasty founded by the labourer's son continued to rule over China for three hundred years, when it was superseded by that of the family to which the present Emperor belongs.

On his accession to the throne Choo took the name of Tae-tsoo, and chose Nanking for his capital, converting Pekin into a principality, which he gave to one of his sons, who, in his turn, when he came to the throne on his father's death, once more made it the chief city of the Empire. The new monarch, Young-lo by name, who had a very able adviser in his wife, inaugurated his reign by restoring many national institutions for which Kublai Khan had substituted those of the Mongols, and Chinese chroniclers tell us he won all hearts by his consideration and moderation. No longer were the chief offices of State held by military men; mandarins were restored to their former rank, and many important privileges were granted to the famous Han-lin College. Whereas Kublai Khan and his successors had encouraged Buddhism, and neglected the teachings of Confucius, Tac-tsoo revived the study of the works of the Chinese sage, forbade women to become priestesses of the Hindu religion, and men to enter convents until they were forty years of age, a truly salutary reform, saving many able natives from wasting the best years of their lives in miserable inactivity.

Speaking of Tac-tsoo, a Chinese historian says: "Every man who knows how to turn circumstances to account, to win a fortune and raise himself above his fellows, must have some merit, but he who from a state of absolute poverty succeeds in working his way to the summit of human greatness, taking his seat on the grandest throne in the world, must indeed be of most extraordinary superiority, worthy to represent Heaven itself as ruler of the human race."

This richly-endowed being did not, however, escape misfortune; before the thirty-one years of his reign were over his favourite son died, and he appointed his grandson, a child of thirteen, to succeed him. The young prince was duly elected to the supreme power; but his uncle, Young-lo, coveted the throne, marched an army to Pekin, and though repulsed at first, was finally successful through the treachery of some soldiers who opened the gates of the capital to him. The palace was set fire to, and the child emperor perished in the flames.

Young-lo was allowed to seat himself on the vacant throne without much opposition; he removed the capital to Pekin, and governed so well that the crimes which had won him power were forgotten. His reign was much disturbed by invasions from the North, the restless Tartars coveting the rich land from which they had been driven out, and at the time it seemed likely that the country would be conquered by them yet again under their great chief Timur, or Tamerlane. Most fortunately for the Celestials, he died on the way to China at the head of his troops, and the land was reprieved for a time at least.

It was during the reign of the usurper Young-lo that a European vessel flying a European flag, that of Portugal, entered a Chinese port. A Portuguese ship had sailed up the Canton river in 1516, and in 1520 a Portuguese Embassy had penetrated to the very gates of Pekin; but its leader, Perez, was sent back a prisoner to Canton, and never heard of again by his fellow-countrymen. He is said, however, to have been beheaded. It was not until the middle of the century that the Portuguese really obtained any footing in the country, but at that time they did succeed in establishing themselves at Macao.

The Ming dynasty was in its turn fated to be overthrown by the restless and ambitious Tartars. The last Emperor of Chinese birth, Whey-tsong, ascended the throne in 1627, but the country was so distracted by internecine feuds that he found the task of government beyond his strength. He committed suicide in his despair at hearing that one of the insurgent leaders had entered Pekin at the head of a large body of soldiers. That leader, Li-Kong by name, had himself proclaimed Emperor, but was only acknowledged by certain provinces, whilst a Chinese general, Woosankwei, made peace with the Manchu Tartars in the name

FIG. 52.—MONOLITHS AT THE ENTRANCE TO THE TOMBS OF THE MING EMPERORS.

of the nation, calling upon them to aid in deposing the usurper. They agreed, all too glad to get an entry into the coveted land they had invaded so often. Li-Kong was expelled, but the Tartar chief, instead of appointing a Chinese monarch, kept the supreme power himself. He was hailed as a deliverer when he entered Pekin, and ordered a grand ceremonial to be observed at his own investiture as Emperor. The Nemesis in store for all traitors was, however, waiting for him; he was taken ill immediately afterwards and died in great agony. Strange to say, his son, Shun-Che, a child of six years old, was allowed to succeed him, and thus in 1644 was founded the dynasty known as the Manchu Tartar, or Ch'ing, which has endured to the present day.

The various provinces of the vast Celestial Empire did not of course submit peacefully to this usurpation, but Ama-van, the uncle of the young monarch, who was appointed regent during his minority, was a man of great ability, who quelled every revolt as it arose. China still bears the traces of the drastic measures employed to restore peace to the distracted land, many a ruined wall marking the site of a once populous town, whilst other cities still standing are evidently but half their original size. The guardian died when his charge was only fourteen; still the young prince had already learnt how to govern, and with a wisdom beyond his years he managed to keep the peace between his Tartar and Chinese subjects, dividing honours and appointments equally amongst members of the two races. It was during the reign of this astute young sovereign that the peculiar style of coiffure which is always looked upon as distinctively Chinese, was first introduced, and that as a sign of subjection to the Tartars. Before the accession of Shun-Che the Celestials had prided themselves on the luxuriance of their

ORIGIN OF THE PIG-TAIL

dark masses of hair, and the issue of an edict ordering all without distinction of age or rank to have their heads shaved, but for one long tress at the back to be plaited into a pig-tail, nearly caused a fresh revolution. The penalty of non-compliance was decapitation, and there were many who chose that rather than the disgrace of submitting to the hands of the barber. Still time,

FIG. 53.—CHINESE BRONZES. (*Univers Pittoresque.*)

the all-healer, has now reconciled the descendants of the innovators to submit to what was originally so detested a custom, and no Chinaman would now feel happy without his pig-tail.

Writing of the Chinese before the hated edict was promulgated, Father Alvarez Semedo says: "Men and women alike let their hair, generally black, grow to a great length, which is why the name of the 'kingdom of the people with black hair' is sometimes given to China. The natives," adds this observer, "have little black eyes and small noses; they think our big prominent noses very ugly; the Chinese look upon them in fact as a regular deformity. They grow very small beards, and do not care for them to be thick, all they are anxious about is that they should be black, which is the most common colour; still they do not object to red hair as the people of Thebes used to do; they wear their hair long, and let it grow just as nature makes it, never cutting it. They give more attention to the arrangement of their coiffure than any other nation of the world; they would rather not have a single hair on their chins than lose one from their polls."

Now the care expended on their luxuriant locks by the ancestors of the modern Chinese is generally concentrated on the once-hated pig-tail; but in the case of old men with grand-children, on long moustaches, and what is known as the pointed Imperial beard. It is very evident that when the Portuguese father quoted above was in China, the Celestials had never seen the English, whom they call the red devils, on account of the auburn hair of so many of them. Had they done so the author would never have said, "They do not object to red hair!"

CHAPTER XIII

The Founder of the Ch'ing dynasty—A broken-hearted widower—The Louis XIV. of China—The Will of Kang-Hy—Young-t-Ching appointed his successor—The character of the new Emperor—Mission of Lord Macartney—He refuses to perform the Ko-too, or nine prostrations—Interview with Young-t-Ching—Results of the Mission to England—Accession of Kien-Long—He resolves to abdicate when he has reigned sixty years—Accession of Taou-Kwang—The beginning of the end—An adopted brother—War against China declared by England—The Pekin Treaty—Prince Hassan goes to visit Queen Victoria—The Regents and Tung-Che—Foreign Ministers compel the young Emperor to receive them.

WE have already, in telling the story of missionary effort in China, referred to the various Emperors of the reigning dynasty who occupied the throne in the seventeenth and eighteenth centuries, but a few further details will be interesting, throwing as they do a light upon the present state of politics in China, where the Empire is tottering to its fall; menaced by invaders, who, though they come preaching peace, will eventually change the country far more completely than did the fire and sword of the Tartar hordes.

The founder of the Ch'ing dynasty died at the early age of twenty-four, of grief, it is said, for the death of a favourite wife, whom he had fallen in love with during her husband's life, and taken to his palace in defiance of every law, human and divine. Certain historians relate, that to pick a quarrel with the rightful spouse of the object of his passion, he gave him a box on the ears which caused him to die of shame. However that may be, the Empress died a few days later; and Shun Che was so distraught with grief that he would have committed suicide but for the restraint put upon him by the eunuchs of his court. According to the revolting custom then still in vogue, he had thirty men strangled on the tomb of the dead Empress to attend her in the other world. He then shaved his head and made pilgrimages from one pagoda to another, bewailing his many sins, especially that of having loved his lost one with too great a love, and pleading for forgiveness. This penance over, he went back to his palace at Pekin. But, says the chronicler, a little time afterwards he called for his Imperial mantle, and having named his son, Kang-Hy, then only eight years old, his successor, he wrapt himself in it and expired with the words, "I go to join my ancestors."

Once more a boy-emperor was raised to the Imperial throne; but that boy was no ordinary child, and grew up to be one of the greatest monarchs who ever ruled the Celestial Empire.

During his minority he was under the care of four wise ministers, who, except for their cruelty to the Christians, performed their difficult task with skill and moderation. One of the very first acts of the young monarch, when he took the reins of government with his own hands, was to rescind the measures against the Christians, placing their religion on exactly the same standing as Buddhism, and consulting the Jesuit fathers at every turn. Many are the touching stories told of the way in which Kang-Hy won all hearts, and some of them read as if they had been culled from the Old Testament. Take, for instance, the tale of the old man, whom the Emperor in one of his royal progresses found weeping by the wayside. Approaching him, Kang-Hy asked the cause of his grief: "My lord," was the reply, "my only son, who was the joy of my life, has been taken from me to serve the governor of the province, and I have no one to comfort me in my old age, or to mourn over my tomb." The Emperor went straight to the Governor's palace, accompanied by the complainant; and when the oppressor could not deny the charge, Kang-Hy ordered him to be beheaded. Then turning to the suppliant the royal avenger thus addressed him: "To make amends to you for the injury you have sustained, I appoint you Governor in the room of him who has proved himself so unworthy of that office."

Missionaries to China were in the habit of calling Kang-Hy the Louis XIV. of China. The contemporary of the *grand monarque* of France, there was really something in his long and brilliant reign not unlike that of the king who acquired an ascendency over his subjects resembling that of an Asiatic autocrat. He knew, as Louis did, how to turn everything to account for the glory of his kingdom, and before his death in 1792 he had so consolidated his power, that but for the weakness of his successors China might still rank as a leader of the Orient. In his will, a quotation from which is given below, he proves alike his literary ability, his care for the best interests of his people, and the exalted view he took of his own duties :

" I, the Emperor," he says, " who honour Heaven, and am charged with the government of the country, I issue this edict, and I assert that amongst the Emperors who have governed the Universe there has not been one who has looked upon the doing reverence to Heaven and imitating his ancestors as essential duties. The true manner to venerate Heaven is to treat those who are far away with goodness, and to advance those who are near according to their merit. This is to procure for the people rest and abundance ; it is to identify one's own well-being with that of the Universe ; it is to preserve the State from dangers before those dangers occur, and to foresee with wisdom the disorders which might occur.

·" The princes who work on this plan from early morning till evening, and are even thinking (of their subjects) during their sleep, who are ceaselessly forming designs, the effects of which will be enduring and of wide influence for the public good, these princes, I say, are not far from the accomplishment of their duties.

"I, Emperor, who am now seventy years old, and have reigned for sixty of them, I owe all my blessings to the invisible aid of Heaven and earth, to that of my ancestors, and to that of the God who presides over the Empire . . . not to my own feeble reason. According to history, more than four thousand three hundred and fifty years have elapsed since the reign of Hwang-Ti, and during that great number of centuries there have been three hundred and one Emperors, a few of whom only have reigned as long as they might have done.

"After my elevation to the throne, when I reached the twentieth year of my reign, I did not dare to count on seeing the thirtieth, and arrived at the thirtieth, I did not dare look forward to the fortieth, yet now find myself in the sixtieth. Happiness is said to consist in five things: long life, wealth, tranquillity, love of virtue, and a peaceful end. The last-named takes the highest rank amongst these advantages, no doubt, because it is so difficult to secure it. The age I now am proves that I have lived a long time; as for my wealth, I have owned all that is in the four seas. I am a father, and have one hundred and fifty sons and grandsons. . . . I have probably even more daughters. . . . I leave the Empire in peace . . . so that the happiness I enjoy may well be called great. . . . If no accident befalls me, I shall die content.

"I have one more reflection to make. Although I cannot claim that since I have been on the throne I have changed all evil customs and reformed the manners of all my people; although I have not succeeded in securing abundance for every family and the necessaries of life to every individual, so that I cannot in these respects be compared to the wise emperors of the first three dynasties, I can assert that during my long reign I have had no other aim than to preserve peace for the whole Empire, to make my people content, each one in his own sphere and profession; it is to this I have devoted assiduous care with incredible ardour and ceaseless toil, which toil has done much to exhaust the strength alike of my body and of my spirit. Amongst my predecessors there were some who reigned but a short time, and historians turn this to account to censure them, attributing their premature death to inordinate love of wine and women. . . . This is quite a regular rule, and they make a merit of raking up stories against accomplished princes who were really the least reprehensible of men."

Kang-Hy then goes on to make an elaborate justification of his predecessors, claiming that their days were shortened by hard work and devotion to duty; he singles out two or three of his own ancestors for special praise, and wanders, as most royal and imperial authors do, into numerous side-issues before he returns to the subject of his own life.

"I, Emperor," he goes on to say, "applied myself to the study of wisdom from infancy, and have acquired a knowledge of ancient and modern science." He adds that when in his full vigour, he could shoot arrows some thirteen cubits long from bows of huge span; that he knew all about the handling of weapons, and had often appeared at the head of his armies in person. He boasts, moreover, that throughout his whole life he had never put any one to death without cause; he had also put down several revolts, and every enterprise in which he had engaged had been conducted in the most successful way by his genius alone.

After thus as it were pronouncing his own funeral oration, he proceeds to appoint his successor in the following terms:

"Young-t-Ching, my fourth son, is a man of rare and valuable character. He greatly resembles me, and I have no doubt he will be capable of bearing the burden of his great inheritance. I ordain that after my death he shall ascend the throne and take possession of the Imperial dignity. In conformity with custom, mourning shall be worn for me for twenty-seven days only. Let this edict be published at Court and in all the provinces, that no one may be ignorant of its contents."

The author of this naïve eulogy of his own

virtues died in 1722, having caught a chill whilst hunting a leopard beyond the Great Wall. As he would himself have wished, his last illness was short; he would have said that his end was peace,

FIG. 54.—PORTRAIT OF ONE OF THE CHINESE EMPERORS OF THE CH'ING DYNASTY, PROBABLY KIEN-LONG.

and that he had achieved the most difficult of the five things which make up human happiness.

The reign of Young-t-Ching, who was duly installed Emperor with all possible pomp after his father's death, was not marked by any special events, and but for his persecution of the Christians, the new monarch seems to have justified the high opinion his predecessor had of him. He died in 1735, and was succeeded by his eldest son, Kien-Long, during whose reign the Chinese Court was visited for the first time by Englishmen, Lord Macartney having been sent in 1792 at the head of a mission to lay the grievances of English merchants before the Emperor and demand redress. This mission was of so much importance to the future relations between the English Government and the Celestial Empire, that some details are given here.

The Embassy was received at Tien-tsin with courtesy, but with no special honour, for in those days none of the officials had any idea that a messenger from a foreign court would come to their country, except to bring tribute and do homage to the Son of Heaven. On the yachts and junks which took the party up the Peiho river were displayed flags bearing the legend, "Ambassadors bearing tribute from the country of England." In his account of the expedition, Sir George Staunton, who edited Lord Macartney's journals, says: "The approach of the embassy was an event of which the report spread rapidly . . . crowds of men assembled on the banks . . . while the females, as shy as they were cautious, looked through gates or peeped over walls to enjoy the sight. A few indeed of the ancient dames almost dipped their feet into the river to get a nearer peep."

It was at Zhehol, about fifty miles north of the Great Wall, where the Emperor had a summer palace, that he consented to receive the ambassador, who was lodged, whilst waiting for the final arrangements to be made, at Yuen-min-Yuen, about seven miles from the capital. A serious hitch occurred in the absolute refusal of Lord Macartney to perform what is known as the ko-too, an act of homage always exacted from a vassal by his liege lord, consisting of nine prostrations at his feet. To have yielded would have been to recognize Kien-Long as the superior of the King of Great Britain, and to Lord Macartney's firmness on this occasion is due all the later success of his fellow-countrymen in the Celestial Empire. Finding him resolute, the President of the Board of Rites and the other great mandarins who had waited upon him, finally consented to a compromise, and the English party, escorted by a guard of Tartars, made their way to Zhehol, where, to quote the words of the ambassador, he saw " King Solomon in all his glory," being received by him in the presence of all the princes of the Imperial family, the great officers of State, the Mongol chiefs, etc., with all courtesy. "The hall of audience," we are told, "was a magnificent tent in the park, supported by gilded pillars, at the upper end of which was placed a throne under a canopy raised several steps from the ground. . . . The Emperor was carried in a palanquin by sixteen bearers, his approach announced by the sound of gongs and trumpets

... he was plainly dressed in a robe of brown silk, with no ornaments but one large pearl in the front of his black velvet cap."

The ambassador, who merely bent one knee in presenting his credentials, was very graciously greeted by the venerable monarch, and when presents had been exchanged, etc., a sumptuous meal was served to the accompaniment of a band of music. The visitors passed a week at Zhehol, and witnessed the festivities in honour of their host's birthday; they were then politely informed that it was time for them to go, and that an answer would be sent to them at Canton to the letter from their King. They were escorted to that sea-port by land and river through the five chief provinces of China, the journey occupying ten weeks, and were greatly struck with the high cultivation of the country and with its teeming population. The promised answer from the Emperor was duly received, and though it did not accede to all the requests made in that of George III., much was gained by the mission, for the trade with England was placed on a far better footing than before.

On his accession to the throne, Kien-Long made the remarkable vow "that should he be permitted ... to complete the sixtieth year of his reign, he would show his gratitude to Heaven by resigning the crown to his heir as an acknowledgment that he had been favoured to the full extent of his wishes." The year after Lord Macartney's visit the allotted period was reached, and the Emperor abdicated in favour of his youngest son, who took the name of Kea-King, and was duly accepted by the Celestials. Kien-Long retained the title of Supreme Emperor until his death at the age of eighty-eight, but he meddled no more in affairs of State, though he continued to aid those who were in distress, winning the name of the Father of his people. He was especially good to the poorer literati, and himself produced several books of high excellence.

Kea-King was, alas! a very different ruler from his father, who had chosen him out of all his children on account of his supposed talent. He had none of the dignity which had characterized the other monarchs of the Manchu dynasty, and chose his friends from amongst the lowest and most depraved of his subjects, taking them with him, it is said, even into the sacred precincts of the Temples when he went to offer sacrifices as the Son of Heaven. It was during the reign of this unworthy scion of a noble house that Lord Amherst was sent to Pekin on a mission similar to that of Lord Macartney. He was not, however, able to see the Emperor, and he and his companions were very rudely treated by the Tartar nobles. The English, on their return home, gave a very far from flattering account of the so-called Celestial court, where they said the whip was largely in use to keep even the great dignitaries in order. The Chinese were then, as they still are, ruled by the whip and the bamboo, for, says a writer who knew the country well, "The viceroy bamboos the mandarins, the mandarins bamboo their inferior officers, and these . . . bamboo the common people; the husband bamboos the wife, the father the son, even when the latter is of mature age."

Before his death Kea-King, who lived to the age of sixty-one, in spite of his excesses, in his turn issued a will in the form of an edict, which contains several interesting passages throwing considerable light on the physical difficulties the authorities have to contend with in the Celestial Empire, as well as on the manners and customs of the people. In it the dying monarch mourns over the devastations caused by "China's sorrow," the Yellow River, and enumerates the measures he had taken to check its ravages. He pronounced, as was usual, an eulogy on his own conduct, and appointed his second son Taou-Kwang his successor.

The name of the new ruler signified the Glory of Reason, and he ascended the throne in 1820. He justified his father's choice by doing all in his power to atone for the mischief done by the weakness and vices of his predecessor, but the chiefs of the unruly Tartar tribes had so got the upper hand that they were beyond his control; one insurrection followed another, and when after making concession after concession, peace was at last restored to the distracted country, a far more formidable enemy had to be contended with from without. The long series of petty quarrels between the English and Celestials on questions of trade culminated in the war already more than once referred to, which lasted for many years, and resulted in the final breaking through of Chinese isolation, and the throwing open of five ports to European trade.

It was the beginning of the end; the first step towards that partition of China which is now being so rapidly effected. Heart-broken at the destruction of all his hopes, Taou-Kwang never held his head up again after the signing of the Treaty of Nanking in 1842. The death of his adopted mother soon afterwards, it is said, hastened his end, and he died in 1851 after a reign of thirty years, during which he had known no peace or comfort.

His fourth son, Yih-Choo, was chosen as his successor, and he took the name of Hien-Fung, signifying universal plenty, but the title turned out a terrible misnomer, for the new Emperor inherited his father's feeble sensual character, and he had not long been on the throne before the Tai-Ping rebellion broke ont. The leader, an able man who had been converted to Christianity, all but succeeded in turning out the Manchu dynasty and inaugurating a new one, with himself as Emperor, under the title of Teen-Wang, or the Heavenly King. To add to the difficulties of Hien-Fung, the English declared war against him in 1857, on account of an outrage on British sailors. The French took part in the campaign, as the allies of the British, and after a struggle lasting three years Pekin itself was entered. Peace was eventually made, on terms very greatly to the advantage of the English, and yet another blow was struck at Chinese prestige by the Treaty of Pekin, signed in 1860. The Tai-Ping rebellion was crushed with the aid of Major Gordon, who afterwards became so celebrated as the Hero of Khartoum, but the Celestials lost more than they gained, and since then the occupant of the throne of the once powerful Empire has been a mere cipher.

Hien-Fung died in 1861, leaving his

FIG. 55.—ONE OF THE REGENTS DURING THE MINORITY OF TUNG-CHE.

enfeebled throne to his infant son, Tung-Che, then only five years old. The government was carried on for him by the so-called Regents, two of the late Emperor's wives, one the legitimate Empress, the other the secondary consort, who did their best to consolidate his power, and seem to have ruled with considerable wisdom and moderation. Rebellion was still, however, rife in the important province of Yunnan, a Mahommedan prince, named Suleiman, still defying the Imperial authority. This leader even sent his son Hassan to England in 1872, to try and obtain the recognition of his father by Queen Victoria. Needless to add, he was not successful, the British Government having already espoused the cause of the young Emperor.

In 1893, the Regents resigned their delegated authority into the hands of Tung-Che, now seventeen years old, but he only reigned two years before he died of small-pox, leaving no children, although he is said to have had two legitimate wives and sixty-nine concubines. His brief term of office was marked by one special event full of significance for foreigners: the various ministers accredited to Pekin, but hitherto not received at the Palace, succeeded in forcing the young monarch to see them in the very stronghold of conservatism.

CHAPTER XIV

A child of four chosen Emperor—The power of the Empress Dowager—The Palace feud—The Palace at Pekin—A Frenchman's interview with the Emperor—The Emperor's person held sacred—Coming of age of the Emperor—An enlightened proclamation—Reception of the foreign ministers in 1889—Education of the young monarch —He goes to do homage at the tombs of his ancestors—A wife is chosen for him—His secondary wives—China, the battle-ground of the future—Railway concessions.

ON the death of the Emperor Tung-Che, there was for the first time for three hundred years no direct heir to the throne of China, and it being the law of the country that the heir must be younger than the person he inherits from, the choice fell upon the infant son of one of Tung-Che's brothers, the Prince of Chun, seventh son of Taou-Kwang, who still occupies the throne, if throne it can be called, when the monarch is a mere prisoner in the hands of the Dowager Empress, compelled to amuse himself in his enforced seclusion as best he can, and spending much of his time in training pets, such as goats and monkeys. The ambitious title of Kwang-Sen, or the "Succession of Glory," was bestowed upon the little fellow of four years old, who has, alas! found his reign rather a succession of misfortunes of every kind than one redounding either to his own glory or that of his people. Once more the unfortunate country has had to suffer all the evils of a long minority, the real power being in the hands of an unscrupulous woman, who yields the sceptre of state with a hand of iron, keeping the "Son of Heaven" in complete subjection. "For many years," says the astute observer, Archibald Colquhoun, in his *China in Transformation*, "the politics of Pekin have been swayed by a bitter Palace feud; the young Emperor and his party on one side, and the Empress Dowager on the other. Of a passionate nature and an imperious will, inspired by purely selfish considerations, the late Regent continues to dominate and even to terrorize the Emperor, who is of feeble physique, and incapable of wielding the power which belongs to him."

He is a mere puppet in the hands of those who ought to obey him, and his name is not associated with a single act of policy worthy of the ruler of a great Empire. Li-Hung-Chang, the courtier, more than once already referred to, is the chief agent of the Dowager Empress, and to these two was due the disgraceful abandonment of the war with Japan—which the Emperor himself wished to carry on to the bitter end—and the signing of the ignominious treaty in 1895. It is just possible that should the Empress Dowager die before him—and she is an old woman now—the Emperor Kwang-Sen may yet take the reins of government into his own hands, but with pretty well every European nation clamouring for a slice of his dominions, he will indeed be a wonderful man if he succeeds in leaving any semblance of power to his successor.

This unfortunate occupant of a doomed throne has spent most of his life at Pekin in the great Palace of his ancestors, his apartments being situated in the centre of the multitudinous buildings, not far from those set apart for the use of the real ruler, the Dowager Empress. The space the Palace occupies is so vast that ministers on their way to the Council Chamber have more than half a mile to walk after entering the precincts. Audience is only given by the Emperor at the early hours, four, five, or six in the morning, and certain high functionaries have the privilege accorded them of being carried to the reception-hall in sedan-chairs. Many an important personage, rejoicing in all manner of high-sounding titles, has however been compelled to remain waiting all night in gala costume in some ante-room, for the early morning interview, and foreigners complain bitterly of the discomforts they still have to endure before they are allowed to come face to face either with the real or the nominal head of the State.

A friend of mine, connected with the French Embassy, told me that on one of the very rare occasions when he and some of his colleagues succeeded in obtaining an interview with the Son of Heaven, the time fixed for the audience was at four o'clock a.m. He was conducted by a chamberlain to a room in which a few candles were burning on a table covered with a yellow cloth. On the other side of this table opposite to him was the Emperor, with a screen of a delicate jonquil-yellow colour on either side. Behind one of these screens knelt Prince Kung, and behind the other the Empress.

Obeying a sign from the chamberlain, the visitors saluted the Emperor, but without performing the ko-too, from which Lord Macartney saved all foreigners by his firm attitude in 1793, and my friend, as he rose up after his respectful obeisance, could not resist just raising his eyes to have a good look at the Son of Heaven, who was at that moment yawning enough to dislocate his jaws. For this presumption the *attaché* was immediately rebuked by the chamberlain, who ordered him to keep his eyes fixed on the ground until the end of the interview.

The Emperor's apartments consist of seven spacious rooms, in each of which is a k'ang or divan, such as is in use everywhere in the north of China, covered with red felt of native manufacture, and provided with cushions adorned with gold embroidery, representing the symbolic dragon and phœnix. On the floors of the royal domain are beautiful European carpets of various kinds, and numerous tables, what-nots, etc., are crowded with objects of art, such as porcelain and pottery, mostly produced in China, though of late years some foreign products have figured amongst them.

The Son of Heaven sleeps in a big bed made at Ning-po, richly decorated with gold and ivory, the very same as that used by his illustrious ancestor Kang-Hy. He is treated by the eight eunuchs in attendance on his person with as much reverence as was the great founder of the now

FIG. 56.—A CHINESE SEDAN-CHAIR AND BEARERS.

weakened dynasty, and as are the Lamas in the convents on the lofty plateaux of Thibet and Mongolia, where the modified form of Buddhism known as Lamaism is practised.

The person of the Emperor is held so sacred that neither iron nor steel is ever allowed to touch him, which of course makes it impossible for him to receive surgical aid should he be suffering from any of the diseases requiring the use of the knife.

Fortunately he was vaccinated when an infant in the cradle, before those in charge of him had any suspicion of the great destiny in store for him. The story goes that a doctor who proposed to save the life of a Chinese Emperor by bleeding him, nearly lost his own head as a punishment. The same superstition prevails in Corea, where one of the kings died in the eighteenth century, when he might have been saved if he, or rather those about him, could have been induced to allow a lancet to be used on his sacred person.

The young Emperor was declared of age in 1889, and he was at once informed that the foreign ministers would be glad to be allowed to pay their respects to him on this auspicious occasion. To their great surprise consent to their reception was given not very long afterwards, that consent being published in the *Pekin Gazette* in the following year in terms most flattering to all concerned. After the usual preamble the Emperor was made to say :

"The ministers of the various powers residing in Pekin have abundantly shown their loyal desire to maintain peaceful relations and international friendship. This I cordially recognize, and I rejoice in it. . . . It is also hereby decreed that a day be fixed every year for an audience ; . . . on the next day the foreign ministers are to be received at a banquet at the Foreign Office. The same is to be done every year in the first month, and the rule will be the same on each occasion. . ."

The remainder of the proclamation was couched in equally courteous terms, presenting a very marked contrast to the grudging, indeed almost insolent, assent given by previous Emperors to any request for an audience by the representatives of the European powers. When the interview took place, moreover, the various ministers were admitted to the presence of their host one by one, instead of all together as on previous occasions, whilst the *attachés*, etc., were received collectively later. The Emperor was seated on a raised platform at the end of the vast reception-hall, with Prince Ching, President of the Foreign Board, kneeling on one side. As each minister came up to the platform making three bows on the way, he was introduced by the Prince, who took from him the letters of credence and placed them on a table near the Son of Heaven, who, after bowing an acknowledgment, made a long speech to the Prince, who listened to it on his knees. The reply completed, he rose, and with uplifted arms went down into the body of the hall, where he repeated to the foreign interpreter the following speech:

"We desire to convey to all the ministers, *chargés d'affaires*, and secretaries, who have presented congratulations to us, that we truly appreciate, and are very pleased with all their kind expressions, and we sincerely wish that their respective sovereigns may this year have all things according to their hearts' desire, and that their happiness and

s

prosperity may increase. We also hope that you ministers will stay long in China in the full enjoyment of health, and that friendly relations between China and foreign countries will never cease."

Surely nothing could be more courteous and conciliatory than the behaviour of the young Emperor on this important occasion, and but for the terrible war with Japan, which so soon afterwards shook his throne to its foundations, he might perhaps have won a real alliance with some Western power, which would have saved him from the partition of his Empire, from which there is now no hope of escape.

On the coming of age of the Son of Heaven, his mother, the Princess of Chun, was raised to the rank of Empress, but his father, the Prince, received no accession of dignity. Both parents, when admitted to the presence of their august son, kneel to him and treat him as a being altogether superior to themselves. Still young, Kwang-Sen is fond of riding, shooting with the bow-and-arrow, and skating. His day is rigidly pertioned out, and he has little real liberty. When he was a child his teachers approached him on their knees, and were only allowed to sit in his presence when he gave them permission. He had to work at the Chinese and Manchu languages for an hour and a half every day, and is really extremely well-educated, though, fortunately for foreigners, he is anything but fond of the mandarins or literati, who would gladly poison his mind against everything European. At

STRINGENT MEASURES OF PRECAUTION

regular intervals he goes to do homage at the tombs of his ancestors, as do all of high or low degree in China, and on these solemn occasions he is accompanied by the Empresses and a suite of no less than thirty thousand persons, including princes, nobles, mandarins, apparitors, lictors, banner-bearers, porters, etc. Long before dawn on the day of the ceremony the main road is strewn with fine sand, and decorated with white and blue velvet flags, whilst at regular intervals tables are set up covered with yellow drapery, and bearing the inscription, *Ya Tao*, signifying the Imperial road, words full of terrible significance to the Chinese, for they mean that all on pain of death should keep out of the way of the Son of Heaven.

The most stringent measures are taken even in the capital to protect the sovereign from the gaze of the profane. Not only are all the inhabitants compelled to close the doors of their houses when he is about to pass, but no one is allowed to climb on the walls of the town, lest from them they should catch even a glimpse of the Imperial procession. Nor is it only reverence for the sacred person which leads to all these precautions: there is the danger that some evil-minded person might attempt to take the life of the Emperor by firing at him from a distance with one of those awful engines of destruction, the range of which even now seems so extraordinary to the Celestials, in spite of their recent experiences in the war with the Japanese. The Chinese police forbid even

European women to show themselves on the day of the procession, lest the sovereign should see them, for the myrmidons of the law, accustomed to the strict seclusion of the female sex in their native land, believe that those who enjoy a liberty such as that of the wives and daughters of the diplomatists, to be capable of any crime even against the venerated Son of Heaven.

A wife was of course chosen for Kwang-Sen as soon as he attained his majority, and the lady selected for the difficult position of Empress was the daughter of an official of the province of Che-kiang, who was, it is said, as good and as well educated as she was beautiful. Truly it must have been an immense change in her life to be raised from her humble position as the child of a mere nobody, to be placed on the throne of the most populous Empire of the world, and the way in which she has fulfilled her high destiny is very differently judged by the few who really know anything of Palace life in China. Her influence

FIG. 57.—A BONZE TORTURING HIMSELF IN A TEMPLE, AFTER A CHINESE PAINTING.
(*Univers Pittoresque.*)

has not of course been as paramount as it would have been in a country where monogamy was practised. Very soon after she became a bride, various supplementary beauties were chosen to fill the royal harem, and the so-called lotus flowers, tea-blossoms, etc., were all equally irreproachable in manners and morals from the Chinese point of view. The number of left-handed marriages permitted in China is illimitable, and where there is money enough to support them, a man often has as many as three hundred secondary wives.

As a matter of course there is none of the fierce jealousy in the Celestial Empire such as is aroused on the mere suspicion of a rival in the virtuous bosom of a European wife. Other countries, other manners; and in China wives and concubines live peacefully enough under one roof, with no more friction than is seen amongst the hens in a poultry-yard. Time alone can show what will be the eventual outcome of the life now being lived in the Imperial Palace of Pekin, for time alone can sift the truth from the many conflicting rumours which reach the outer world. One thing alone is certain, China will be the battle-ground of the future, and the yellow peril, about which so much has been prophesied, will assume many an unexpected form before the century just about to begin in its turn nears its close.

CONCLUSION

WHEN every month brings some change in the political position in China, and the daily press is full of more or less contradictory rumours as to what is going on at Pekin, it is impossible to come to any real decision on the many vexed questions under discussion. One great fact, however, emerges distinctly from out of the chaos of conflicting data, and that is, that it will be Russia, with her wonderful faculty for working steadily onwards towards a definite aim, who will secure the lion's share in the spoliation of the Celestials, whilst her Trans-Siberian railway, which already pays its way, creating trade wherever it passes, and in another four years will connect St. Petersburg with Port Arthur, will be one of the most important factors in changing the course of the commerce of the world.

Shut in as she is on the East by the English in Burmah and the French in Cochin-China, threatened on the West by the Germans and the Japanese, and dominated on the north by Russia, the Celestial Empire finds herself compelled to awake from her long stupor, and to arouse herself to action of some kind. With no real army, no longer an efficient fleet, however, what can she do? She can only choose what seems to her the least of the evils hemming her in on every side, and elect from among the many competitors for the post, the protector best able to save her not only from her outside enemies, but from herself.

As has been very aptly said, Russia is of all the Western Powers the most imbued with Oriental ideas, and she combines, with the energy and ambition of a first-rate power of the future, a sympathy with the Celestials altogether wanting to France, Germany, or Great Britain. There is, in fact, an actual affinity of race between the Chinese and the inhabitants of the northern steppes, and there is therefore far more hope of real amalgamation between them than there can be in any other case. The English, the French, the Germans, the Italians, if they win the concessions they are now in their turn clamouring for, will always be aliens in the districts they acquire, and there will never, to use a homely but expressive phrase, be any love lost between them and the natives.

Li-Hung-Chang, one of the most enlightened statesmen who have ever arisen in China, came to Europe in 1896 with a view to ascertaining by personal observation, which of the western nations would be likely to be the best friend for his distracted country, in the enfeebled condition to which the war with Japan had reduced her. He saw quickly enough that it would not be England, nor Germany, nor France, but that it would be Russia. It was therefore with Russia that a treaty was eventually made, and ratified in 1897; this treaty, in addition to other privileges, giving to the great northern power, Port Arthur, with the right of making it a coaling station, and in case of war of concentrating troops in its harbour. "The Russians and the Chinese," said Mitchie, writing more than thirty years ago, "are peculiarly suited to each other . . . the Russians meet the Chinese as Greek meets Greek . . . they understand each other's character thoroughly, because they are so closely alike." Recent events have proved how true was the insight of this astute observer, and it is evident that whilst the other Powers will have to content themselves with their various spheres of influence, Russia alone will obtain real political control of the Celestial Empire as a whole. There remains now no hope that the disintegrating forces at work in the once powerful nation will be arrested from within, in spite of the fact that again and again China has risen in the past from apparent dissolution into a greater nation than before, absorbing her conquerors and converting them into patriots, ready to dare all for their adopted country. The saving force must now come from without, and when once more there is a strong hand directed by a strong brain at the head of

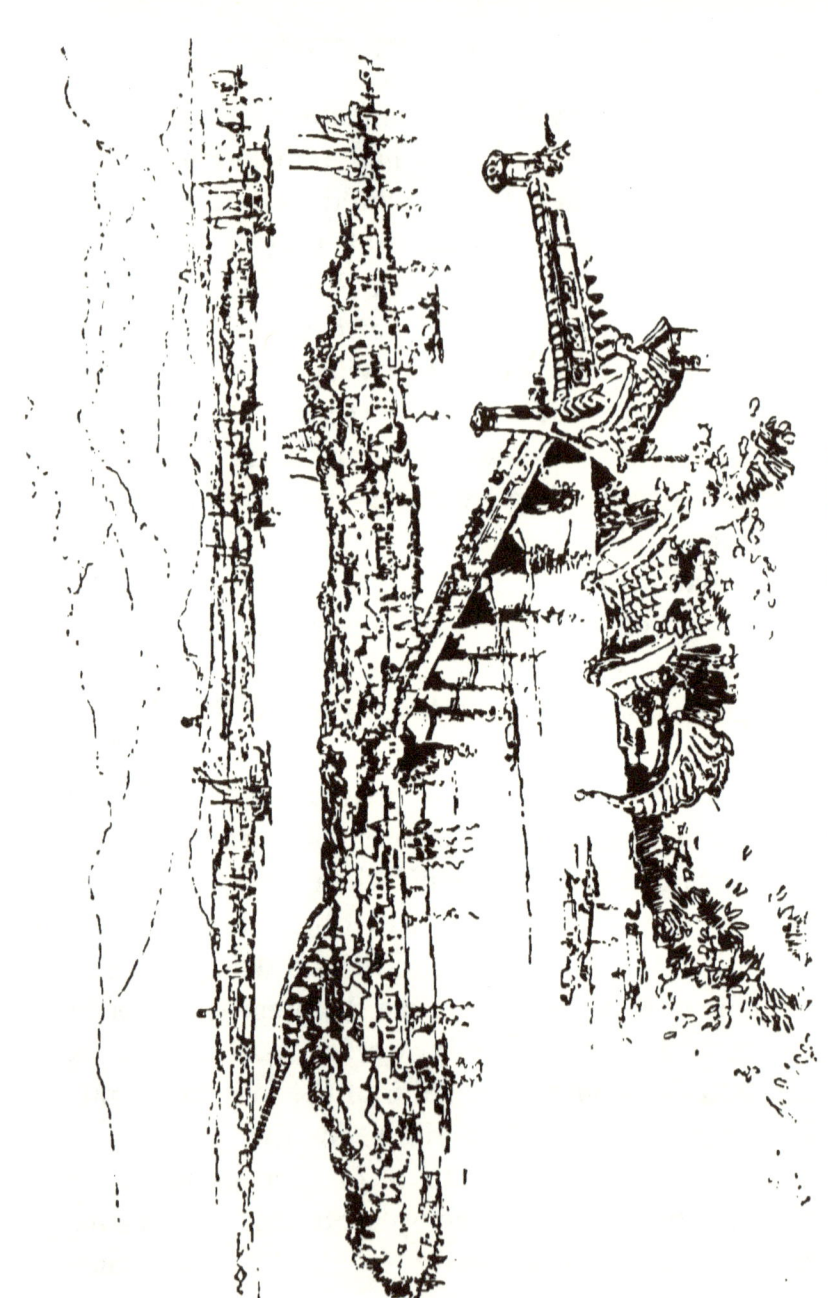

FIG. 58.—THE TOWN AND BRIDGE OF FUCHAN.

affairs, the resources of the unhappy land will be found to be practically inexhaustible. With a prolific soil, vast mineral wealth, and a teachable population, there is indeed no limit to what China, which has been called the India of the future, may become.

In the imminent partition of China into spheres of influence, should that partition finally supersede the more generous policy of the opening of the whole country on equal terms to the trade of all the European nations, the Yang-tse basin, with its populous towns of Nanking, Hankow, Fuchan, and others, will be the field of action of Great Britain; whilst Shantung, a rich sea-bound province, will be that of Germany; and the French, who already occupy Tonking on the south, will obtain concessions in the neighbouring districts. On every side railways are now being projected, and the probability is that ere the century just about to open has run half its course, the whole of China will be intersected by them.

In the Blue Book on Chinese affairs, issued on the 14th March of the current year (1899), the following significant statistics of the railway concessions granted to foreigners in the Celestial Empire are given, showing that Great Britain is more than equal to Russia in the actual amount of mileage secured, whilst Germany, France, Belgium, and America have among them less than Great Britain alone:

British railways	2800	miles.
Russian „	1,530	„
German „	720	„
Belgian „	650	„
French „	420	„
American „	300	„

More important still, as breaking up finally the isolation on which China has prided herself for so many centuries, is the fact that already pretty well all the important towns of the vast Empire are connected by telegraph with each other, and with the outside world. The search-light of publicity is in fact turned full upon the land once so fraught with mystery, and before long there will be no hidden thing connected with either court or country which will not be revealed to the inquisitive gaze of all the world.

THE END